Ancient Worlds
Modern Beads

Ancient Worlds Modern Beads

MORTIRA NATASHA VANPELT

BARRON'S

Ancient Worlds Modern Beads

First edition for North America published in
2015 by Barron's Educational Series, Inc.

All inquiries should be addressed to:
Barron's Educational Series, Inc.
250 Wireless Boulevard
Hauppauge, New York 11788
www.barronseduc.com

ISBN: 978-1-4380-0657-4

Library of Congress Control No.:
2014951592

QUAR.M ACB

Conceived, edited, and designed by
Marshall Editions
The Old Brewery
6 Blundell Street
London N7 9BH
www.marshalleditions.com

© 2015 Marshall Editions

Senior editor: Katie Crous
Art editor & designer: Jackie Palmer
Art director: Caroline Guest
Picture researcher: Sarah Bell
Illustrator: Kuo Kang Chen
Copy editor: Ruth Patrick
Proofreader: Claire Waite Brown

Creative director: Moira Clinch
Publisher: Paul Carslake

Color separation in Hong Kong by
  Cypress Colors (HK) Ltd.
Printed in China by Hung Hing Off-set
  Printing Co. Ltd

9 8 7 6 5 4 3 2 1

Contents

Introduction

Three of the most enduring and influential cultures in human history, Ancient Egypt, Greece, and Rome continue to inspire and amaze us after thousands of years. Though much of our current culture can be traced back to these roots, it is the lasting artifacts—and new archaeological discoveries—that we turn to for inspiration. From jewelry to mosaics and sculpture, the remnants of the classical world capture our imaginations time and again.

Jewelry designers around the world continue to reinvent the styles and techniques of the ancient elite, and the popularity of bold statement jewelry allows even the most elaborate pieces to have their place in today's jewelry box. As modern beaders, we have the advantage of an endless variety of affordable and inspiring beads with which to create. With the 30 projects in this book, my aim is to connect popular beadweaving techniques with ancient themes, combining the styles of genuine artifacts and the essence of ancient art with tiny seed beads.

I have compiled some of my favorite designs for necklaces, bracelets, earrings, and rings that will provide both new and experienced beaders with a gorgeous palette of techniques for jewelry making. I like to take a metal-free approach to jewelry design, so in the following pages you'll find step-by-step instructions for some of my favorite beaded clasps and clasp-free designs. Once you've mastered the techniques, experiment with these projects and incorporate your own favorite beads and findings to forge a wearable link to the past.

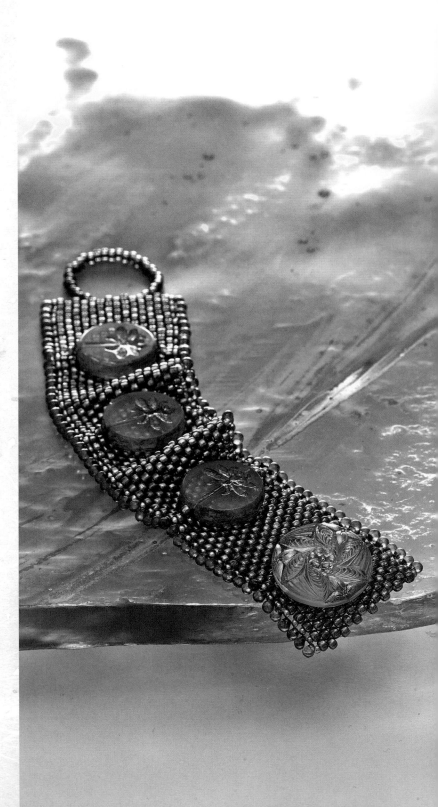

About This Book

Projects:

ANCIENT EGYPT, PAGES 14–51
ANCIENT GREECE, PAGES 52–91
ANCIENT ROME, PAGES 92–129

Guiding you through three of the most influential periods of history, this book offers a stunning array of jewelry projects—from necklaces and collars to cuffs and rings—based on treasured artifacts from the relevant eras and empires. Taking advantage of the wealth of beautiful beads available to today's beader, you will learn how to recreate and give a modern a twist to original designs from the past.

Materials, Tools, and Core Techniques PAGES 8–13 AND 130–139

Turn to the relevant pages toward the front of this book for an overview of the beader's essential materials and tools, and how to use them. The Core Techniques toward the back of the book will help you complete the projects, with clear instructions for key stitches and knots.

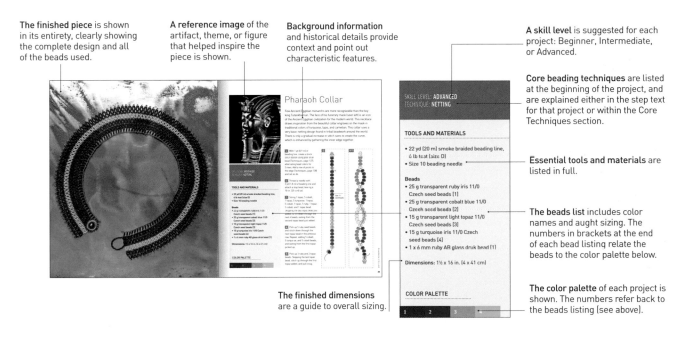

The finished piece is shown in its entirety, clearly showing the complete design and all of the beads used.

A reference image of the artifact, theme, or figure that helped inspire the piece is shown.

Background information and historical details provide context and point out characteristic features.

A skill level is suggested for each project: Beginner, Intermediate, or Advanced.

Core beading techniques are listed at the beginning of the project, and are explained either in the step text for that project or within the Core Techniques section.

Essential tools and materials are listed in full.

The beads list includes color names and aught sizing. The numbers in brackets at the end of each bead listing relate the beads to the color palette below.

The finished dimensions are a guide to overall sizing.

The color palette of each project is shown. The numbers refer back to the beads listing (see above).

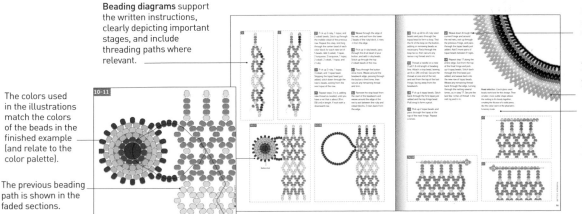

Beading diagrams support the written instructions, clearly depicting important stages, and include threading paths where relevant.

The colors used in the illustrations match the colors of the beads in the finished example (and relate to the color palette).

The previous beading path is shown in the faded sections.

Detailed step instructions guide you through each stage of making the project.

A color variation is included for many projects to inspire you to create your own palettes and patterns.

Useful professional tips are scattered throughout, helping you to overcome any specific challenges and ease the jewelry-making process.

Materials

Listed below are the basics of what you'll need to create the jewelry featured in this book, but don't stop here! When you're ready to experiment, you can incorporate all of your favorite beads into the designs for unique new looks.

NYLON BEADING THREADS

Soft and supple nylon beading threads are typically sold on small spools in a wide variety of colors. There are many sizes or thicknesses available, but for the projects in this book we'll be using a standard size D. Nylon beading thread must be stretched before working it to prevent the beadwork from relaxing and becoming loose after it is complete. After cutting the required length, stretch each length of thread you will use by pulling it taut gently with both hands.

For beadweaving projects, you'll also need to condition the thread with beeswax or a microcrystalline wax. Simply press the thread against the conditioner of your choice and gently pull it through to coat it. Repeat two or three times for a heavier coat. Wipe away any excess wax before you begin weaving. For fringes and tassels, leave the thread unwaxed for a supple texture.

BRAIDED BEADING LINE

This alternative to nylon beading threads is in fact a type of fishing line. Not to be confused with clear monofilament, this braided line is made of several woven fibers for a thread-like texture. Because it is polyethylene based, the thread grips beads snugly and creates sturdy beadwork. Beading line can be bought in a handful of colors and sizes and is ready to use right off the spool. For the projects in this book, you'll need the standard 6 lb test (size D) in smoke gray and crystal white.

Braided beading lines do not need to be stretched or conditioned, but a light coat of wax can help to prevent tangling if you're working with more than a wingspan length at a time. Smoke- or black-colored lines can have a powdered coating that will come off on your fingers while working; although it is harmless, the powder can stain matte-finished beads. If desired, run your line through a tissue or cloth before you thread on a needle to remove most of the excess powder coating.

BEADING CORD

Often used for pearl knotting, this heavier thread for bead stringing comes in nylon or silk. Some varieties are sold on spools, while others are sold on thread cards and will often have a flexible wire needle attached for ease of use. Available in several thicknesses, beading cord does not need conditioning, but you may need to stretch or relax your cord if the thread card has left kinks.

WAXED COTTON CORD

This soft and flexible beading cord is ideal for a variety of mixed-media projects, and for creating sliding knot jewelry. Waxed cord is available in a variety of sizes and colors, with basic colors sold in affordable bulk spools. For the projects ahead, you can also use waxed linen or leather cord in place of cotton.

FINDINGS

Most of the projects in this book feature handmade clasps, but you will need a few findings to round out your stash.

Earwires come in a wide variety of styles and metals, so you can match them to the colors and themes of your earring projects. You'll also need jump rings in a matching metal or finish to attach them. To open, grasp the jump ring with two pairs of round- or flat-nose pliers on either side of the seam, then gently twist—don't pull the ends outward, as this will warp the ring. Repeat in reverse to close, making sure that the ends are flush together.

Shank buttons—with a single loop or hook at the back—are also used throughout the book. The projects ahead all feature designer Czech glass buttons; feel free to substitute your favorites, but look for pieces that closely match the recommended button size in each project.

6 lb test (size D) braided
beading line

Size D black nylon
beading thread

Natural beeswax
thread conditioner

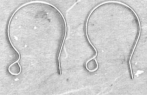

Silk beading cord

Silver filled French earwires

Czech glass designer button

Antique copper basic earwires

Vintage glass buttons

Waxed cotton cord

Jump rings

Vintage face buttons

BEADS

Although many types of beads were present in the jewelry of all three of the cultures we'll be exploring, ancient beads weren't quite as amazing and varied as they are today. Thanks to readily available materials and modern production methods, today's creative beader can choose between millions of bead varieties to suit any project.

SEED BEADS

Round glass seed beads—or rocailles— are the essential building blocks for beadweaving projects. These tiny beads are made in Japan and the Czech Republic by cutting short lengths from long glass tubes and tumbling them until the edges are smooth. Czech seed beads can vary somewhat in size and are generally donut shaped. Japanese seed beads—not to be confused with the more precise cylinder beads or Delicas—are slightly larger and have a more uniform barrel shape.

Some of the projects in this book will call for a specific make of seed bead to achieve a particular effect; otherwise, please feel free to use your favorite brand. The quantities given for seed beads are approximate; it's a good idea to have twice the amount you think you'll need to allow for spills and flawed beads.

Size 11 (or 11/0) seed beads are the most common size used, but you will also find projects in the following pages for tiny size 15 (15/0) seed beads, plus larger size 8 (8/0) and size 6 (6/0) seed beads. Remember that the larger the number, the smaller the beads will be.

SHAPED SEED BEADS

In addition to the common round seed bead, many manufacturers also offer a wide variety of shaped seed beads to add texture and dimension to beadweaving projects. There are drops and fringe beads, two-hole beads of varying shapes, cubes, triangles, O-shaped spacers, and many more.

GLASS BEADS

Pressed glass beads from the Czech Republic are very affordable and come in a dazzling array of shapes, colors, and finishes. From the simple smooth glass druk (Czech for "round"), to elaborate coins and natural shapes, glass accent beads are perfect for adding unique embellishments and focal points to beadwork.

Picasso finish is a coating added to glass beads that gives them a faux antique or marbled look. The finish can greatly affect the look of the base color, from man-made to organic, making Picasso glass an affordable substitute for precious gems in classically inspired beadwork.

ARTISANAL AND TRADE BEADS

Imported and vintage glass beads from around the world offer a fantastic way to add elements of ancient or tribal appeal to your beadwork. The organic shapes and bold colors are instantly appealing, and can add a bit of history, too. White-heart beads— made from a layer of transparent glass over a white core—provide an intense splash of color unmatched by other bead types.

Be sure to wash glass trade beads thoroughly in plain water and allow them to dry overnight before weaving with them.

NATURAL BEADS

Bone, horn, shell, and pearl beads make for gorgeous accents in beadwork. You can also find a wide variety of beads made from seeds and other organic materials to add an earthiness to your designs. Many types of natural beads are made by small groups of artisans using materials and techniques unique to their region. These beads can add a lot of personality to your work.

Freshwater pearls should always be removed from the strand and washed gently in plain water before use.

SEED BEADS

Size 8 AB (Aurora Borealis) finish Japanese seed beads

Size 8 transparent Czech seed beads

Size 11 matte Japanese seed beads

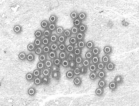

Size 11 Ceylon Czech seed beads

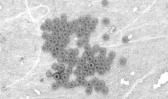

Size 15 opaque Japanese seed beads

SHAPED SEED BEADS

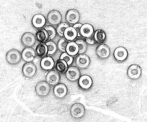

Picasso finish rice drops

AB finish O-shaped spacers

Picasso finish fringe drops

Picasso finish two-hole tube beads

Opaque two-hole duo beads

Opaque dagger beads

ARTISANAL AND TRADE BEADS

Java glass rondelles

Striped Java glass beads

White-heart trade beads

African Christmas beads, or love beads

Ancient Roman glass disk

GLASS BEADS

AB finish pressed fish beads

Egyptian cartouche tile bead

Tortoiseshell finish coins

Picasso finish three-dot ovals

Picasso finish round druk beads

NATURAL BEADS

Baroque freshwater pearls

Dyed wood Heishi bead spacers

Wood tube beads

Natural bone rounds

Dyed semi-round freshwater pearls

Buri nut beads

Tools

Every beader needs a few essential tools to get the job done, and some extras to make beadwork just a little easier. You don't need to purchase expensive tools to get good quality, but cheap tools can give you poor results in finishing your projects. Whether you spend a little or a lot, be sure to use and store your tools with care so they will last a long time. To keep your tools in good repair, use them only for beading projects.

BEADING NEEDLES

Needles made specifically for beadwork have a small and narrow eye that can pass through most beads several times. Two basic lengths are available: long needles make it easy to pick up multiple seed beads at once, while short needles or sharps are comfortable to use for long periods. Use whichever needle length suits you best. Flexible wire beading needles are also useful for stringing beads on heavier cord that won't pass through your regular needle's eye.

To complete the projects in this book you'll need standard size 10 needles, and size 13 for the smallest of beads. Size 13 needles also come in handy when you encounter a bead that simply can't take another pass with the standard-size needle. Never try to force a needle through a bead—it will probably shatter and ruin all of your hard work.

Because beading needles are so thin, they will curve over time and can break under too much tension. Be sure to have at least two of each size you need before starting a project.

SCISSORS AND PLIERS

There are many styles of scissors and snips available for beadweaving. Choose a pair of scissors with small blades to get in close to the beadwork to trim tails. To keep the blades sharp, always use a separate pair of scissors for thread— and don't give them double duty cutting fabric or paper. If you use both nylon and braided threads frequently, you may want to invest in a separate pair of cutting tools for each. Thread burners and even good-quality nail clippers are also great for trimming braided lines neatly.

Two pairs of simple round- or flat-nose pliers are all you need to complete the projects in this book.

GLUE

Many beading techniques and projects require a little extra adhesive help from glues, lacquers, or Epoxy. To complete some of the designs in this book, you may want to add some clear nail polish to your stash for sealing knots or reinforcing bead loops.

RULERS

Measuring your beadwork is essential to achieve the right fit or drape, so have at least one measuring tool in your workspace. A flexible measuring tape is ideal, particularly if it is on a retractable spool for easy winding. You may also want to invest in a ring mandrel for sizing and shaping rings. A bracelet sizing cone can help achieve the perfect length, no matter the design of the bracelet.

EXTRAS

The odds and ends that make your workspace unique and comfortable will vary depending on how and where you do your beading. A few extra tools to consider include containers, trays, and scoops for sorting and mixing beads, and small dishes to hold the beads you are currently working with. You'll also need containers to store your tools and materials, but don't feel that you have to make a big investment on these. Your storage methods will evolve as your bead tastes do.

Size 10 long
beading needles

Size 13 long
beading needles

Flexible wire
needle

Bead storage jar

Miniature bead tin

Round-nose pliers

Bead scoop

Beading scissors

Clear nail polish

Thread nipper tool

Retractable tape

Ring mandrel

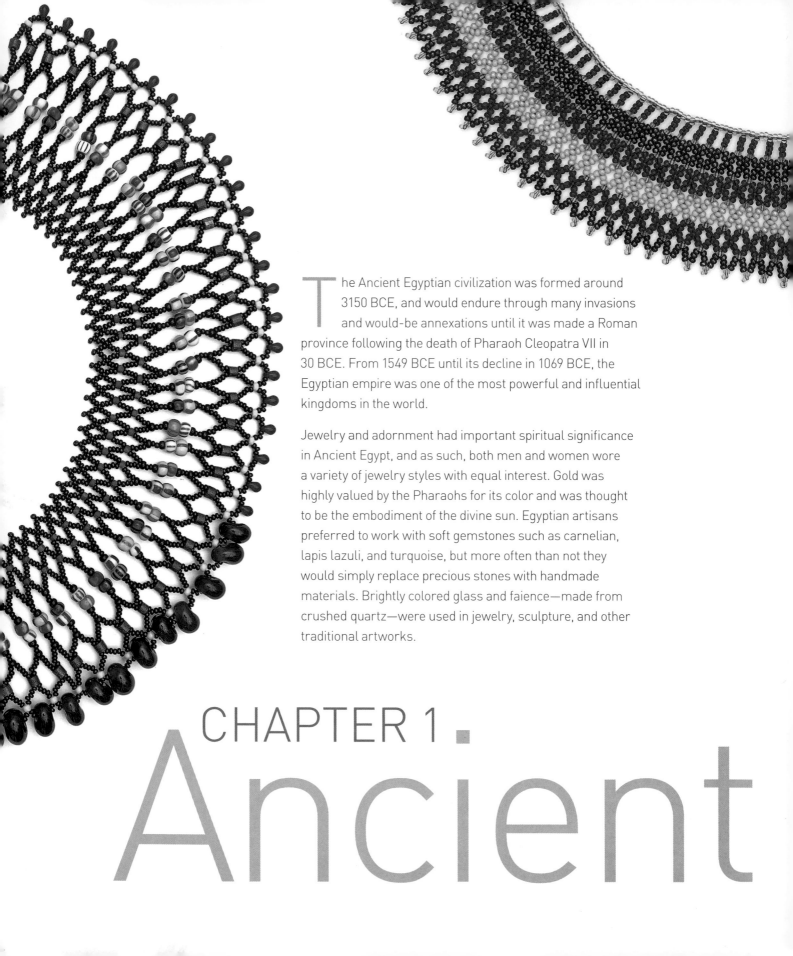

The Ancient Egyptian civilization was formed around 3150 BCE, and would endure through many invasions and would-be annexations until it was made a Roman province following the death of Pharaoh Cleopatra VII in 30 BCE. From 1549 BCE until its decline in 1069 BCE, the Egyptian empire was one of the most powerful and influential kingdoms in the world.

Jewelry and adornment had important spiritual significance in Ancient Egypt, and as such, both men and women wore a variety of jewelry styles with equal interest. Gold was highly valued by the Pharaohs for its color and was thought to be the embodiment of the divine sun. Egyptian artisans preferred to work with soft gemstones such as carnelian, lapis lazuli, and turquoise, but more often than not they would simply replace precious stones with handmade materials. Brightly colored glass and faience—made from crushed quartz—were used in jewelry, sculpture, and other traditional artworks.

CHAPTER 1.
Ancient

The Ancient Egyptians wore many types of jewelry, including necklaces, rings, brooches, and earrings. The importance of jewelry in warding off spirits or communing with deities also contributed to the invention of jewelry designs unique to the region. Pectoral amulets, with elaborate cloisonné style tableaux, and beaded wesekh broadcollars are the most recognizable signature jewelry styles of Ancient Egypt.

In this chapter, we'll explore combining classic Egyptian color palettes with beadwork techniques to create stunning statement jewelry. Some traditional patterns and motifs from Ancient Egypt are recreated using essential beadweaving stitches and modern bead styles for a treasure trove of wearable art.

Egypt

Scarab Ring

The scarab beetle was one of the most sacred creatures in Ancient Egypt, and was depicted often in jewelry, such as the gold ring seen here. This beaded ring project captures the wonderful metallic green of a natural beetle shell, with a pretty striped focal point. It is a cinch to stitch, and a great way to practice peyote stitch. If you don't yet have a ring sizing mandrel in your tool stash, you'll need a dowel or other tube to stretch your ring to the correct size.

SKILL LEVEL: **BEGINNER**
TECHNIQUE: **PEYOTE STITCH**

TOOLS AND MATERIALS

- 1¾ yd (1.5 m) smoke braided beading line, 6 lb test (size D)
- Size 10 beading needle
- Ring sizing mandrel (optional)

Beads
- 2 g gold lustered emerald 11/0 Japanese seed beads (1)
- 30 metallic olivine 11/0 Japanese seed beads (2)
- 10 opaque black 11/0 Japanese seed beads (3)

Dimensions: ½ x 2 in. (1.2 x 5 cm)

Matching sets: The simple motif in this ring makes it easy to match to other projects, such as the Valley of the Queens Cuff (page 34) and the Jeweled Collar (page 24).

COLOR PALETTE

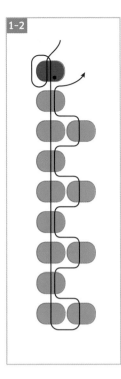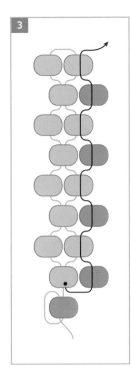

1 Attach a stop bead to 1¾ yd (1.5 m) of beading line, leaving a 6-in. (15-cm) tail. Pick up 8 emerald beads, and slide them down the thread. Turn the stop bead away from you.

2 Pick up 1 emerald bead. Skipping the last bead added, stitch up through the next bead, and pull snug. Repeat 3 times.

3 Turn the beadwork. Pick up 1 emerald bead, and stitch up through the first raised bead of the previous row. Repeat 3 times.

4 Continue adding 4 beads per row with peyote stitch until you have a strip that is 12 beads wide. On the next row, add 1 olivine, 1 black, and 2 olivine beads (a). Repeat until the pattern is 5 beads wide (b).

5 Add 4 emerald beads per row until the peyote strip is 2 rows or 1 ring size shorter than the desired length. The beadwork will stretch by one size once complete, so it is important to finish a little short for a good fit.

6 Bring the short edges together. Pass the needle through the raised bead directly opposite from where your thread is exiting. Gently pull snug.

7 Pass through the next raised bead in the opposite row. Repeat to join the edges together, then weave back across the join to close.

8 Weave in all remaining thread and trim. Place the ring over a ring-sizing mandrel or dowel and stretch it gently to the correct size.

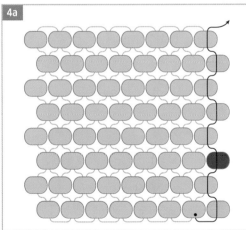

Variations: If you prefer not to leave your threads exposed at the beadwork edges, make your ring to the desired size before zipping it up, then add a round of circular square stitch after connecting the edges (Techniques, page 138). The trim will allow for less stretch than a plain peyote band.

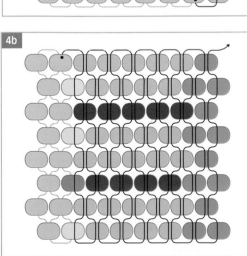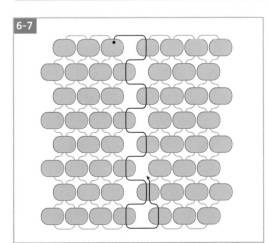

Securing your beadwork: When weaving in your threads, work one bead at a time and use light tension to prevent warping in the beadwork.

Nile Necklace

When we think of Egyptian necklaces, the broad collar or wesekh is often the first thing that comes to mind. In fact, the strung necklace was a very common style worn by many Egyptians, from royalty to craftsmen. This project uses a combination of traditional Egyptian colors and a few select bead shapes to recreate the look of an authentic Egyptian necklace. Pieces like the simple pectoral amulet shown left have been found in large collections, buried with wealthy Ancient Egyptians.

SKILL LEVEL: BEGINNER
TECHNIQUE: STRINGING

TOOLS AND MATERIALS

• 40 in. (1 m) black silk or nylon beading cord, 0.6 mm (Size 4)
• Sewing needle or twisted wire needle
• Clear nail polish or jeweler's glue

Beads
• 2 x 14 mm green Czech glass fish beads (1)
• 3 x 14 mm red Czech glass scarab beads (2)
• 6 x 9.5 mm dark blue glass teardrop beads (3)
• 27 x 4 mm red natural horn round beads (4)
• 33 x 4 mm amber natural horn beads (5)
• 6 g opaque cobalt blue 8/0 seed beads (6)

Dimensions: 26 in. (66 cm)

COLOR PALETTE

1	2	3	4
5	6		

3

Size 8 seed beads

Teardrop bead

Glass fish bead

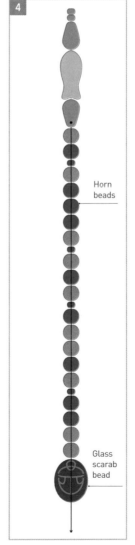

4

Horn beads

Glass scarab bead

1 Stretch or relax your beading cord if necessary and secure one end to your workspace with a bit of tape. Thread the opposite end with your needle of choice.

2 Divide your red and amber horn beads into roughly equal halves and create two mixes with both colors. Set one half of the beads aside.

3 String about 5½ in. (14 cm) of size 8 blue seed beads. Add 1 teardrop, 1 fish bead, and 1 teardrop, with the wide ends of each facing the fish bead.

4 String horn beads and size 8 blue seed beads at random for about 3½ in. (9 cm). Add 1 scarab bead, with the eyes toward the fish bead.

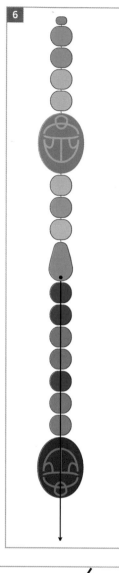

5 String 1 amber bead, 1 red bead, 1 amber bead, and 1 teardrop with the narrow end toward the scarab.

6 Add horn beads for about 1¼ in. (3 cm) and then 1 scarab bead.

7 Repeat the pattern in reverse, starting with 1¼ in. (3 cm) of horn beads, making sure to string the next scarab bead facing upward, and finish with size 8 seed beads.

8 Remove the tape from your cord end and center all of the beads on the strand. Tie a square knot as close to the beads as possible (a), then secure it with an overhand knot over the top (b). Dab the knots with a small amount of clear nail polish or jeweler's glue and allow to dry.

9 On one tail thread, string a red horn bead and 1 size 8 seed bead. Tie 3 overhand knots as close together as possible, about 1 in. (2.5 cm) from the main beadwork. Dab the knot with nail polish or glue, and allow to dry.

10 Repeat on the other tail thread, using an amber bead. Once all the knots are dry, trim any remaining thread from the tails.

Project planning: The Ancient Egyptians used many different types of beads in their necklaces, and you can make an authentic-looking piece with a variety of materials you might have in your bead stash. Start with a few earthy colors, jewel tones, shapes from nature, and organic textures, and build your palette from there.

Bead selection: If you can't find fish or scarabs, other animal or even plant shapes will work as well. You can also go for a more modern or understated look with tubes, daggers, or disks.

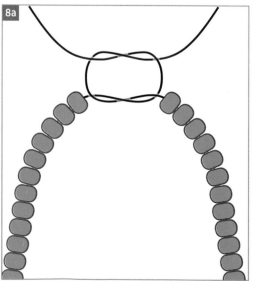

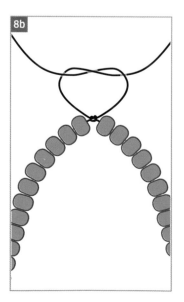

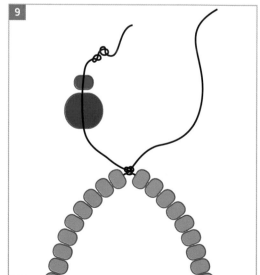

Amarna Earrings

In Ancient Egypt, big and bold earrings were worn by both men and women. These colorful hoop earrings are inspired by bold glass ear adornments found in the ancient city of Amarna, home of Pharaoh Akhenaten and his wife Nefertiti, seen here in the famous sculpture. Combining two bead sizes with right-angle weave creates the perfect curve to make the earrings hold their round shape. The tube will fit perfectly into a standard jump ring when zipped together, so your spiky accents will stay in place.

SKILL LEVEL: **INTERMEDIATE**
TECHNIQUE: **RIGHT-ANGLE WEAVE (RAW)**

TOOLS AND MATERIALS

- 2 x 20-gauge (0.8-mm) 6 mm silver filled jump rings
- 2 x 20-gauge (0.8-mm) 6 mm silver filled French earwires
- 4 yd (3.6 m) smoke braided beading line, 6 lb test (size D)
- Size 10 and 13 beading needles

Beads
- 3 g turquoise luster 11/0 Czech seed beads (1)
- 2 g lemon yellow 11/0 Czech seed beads (2)
- 3 g opaque turquoise 15/0 seed beads (3)
- 4 black 2.5 mm rice drops (4)
- 4 white 2.5 mm rice drops (5)

Dimensions: 1¾ x 1 in. (4.5 x 2.5 cm)

COLOR PALETTE

1	2	3
4	5	

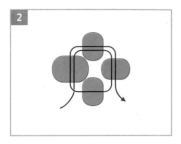 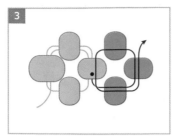 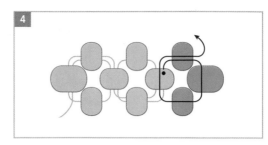

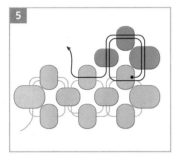 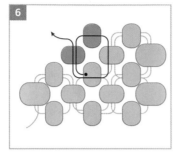 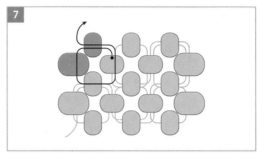

1 Thread a needle on a 2-yd (1.8-m) length of beading line. Pick up 1 turquoise size 11 bead and 3 size 15 beads. Slide them down to the end, leaving a 6-in. (15-cm) tail.

2 Stitch up through the first 2 beads just added, and pull snug. Stitch down through the following bead.

3 Pick up 3 size 15 seed beads and stitch down through the same bead that your thread is exiting. Pull snug to form a new RAW cluster, then stitch through the first 2 beads just added.

4 Pick up 1 size 15, 1 turquoise size 11, and 1 size 15. Stitch up through the bead that your thread is exiting and pull snug. Pass through the first bead just added.

5 Pick up 1 size 11 and 2 size 15 beads. Stitch through the bead that your thread is exiting and pull snug. Pass through all 3 beads just added and

the next raised bead from the previous row.

6 Pick up 2 size 15 beads, and stitch down through the third bead added in the previous stitch, the raised bead from the previous row, and the first bead just added.

7 Pick up 1 size 15 and 1 size 11 bead. Stitch through the raised bead in the previous row to close the cluster. Pass through the following 2 beads to exit from the size 15 bead just added. Turn the beadwork so the thread is on the right.

8 Repeat steps 5 to 7 for 27 rows, to create a strip that has 29 turquoise size 11 seed beads along either side. Pass through the size 11 added in the final stitch.

9 Open a jump ring and thread on 1 earwire. Close the jump ring. Thread a needle on the tail thread and pass it through the jump ring. Pinch the edges of the RAW strip together, and pass

6 rows of beadwork through the jump ring.

10 Bring the short edges of the beadwork together, and pass the tail thread through the nearest size 15 bead on the edge.

11 Pick up 1 size 15 bead, and pass through the size 15 on the opposite edge. Pick up 1 turquoise size 11, and pass through the first size 15 again.

12 Stitch through the next 2 beads to exit the following size 15 on the edge. Add 1 size 15 and 1 turquoise size 11 to complete the RAW pattern. Weave through the join once to secure, weave in all remaining tail thread, and trim.

13 Pick up the working thread again and pick up 1 turquoise size 11 seed bead. Pass through the size 11 seed bead on the opposite edge.

14 Pick up 1 yellow size 11 seed bead, and stitch through the first size 11 bead on the edge again, the turquoise size 11 just added, and the next size 11 on the edge.

Stitch help: This project can be a bit tricky if you are not familiar with either RAW or size 15 seed beads. Take it slowly, and watch your stitches carefully, making sure that you're always moving in a figure-eight pattern. Each row should always have 3 raised beads across the top, with 4 horizontal beads below.

8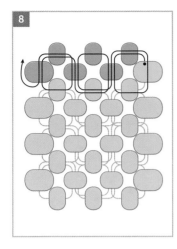

9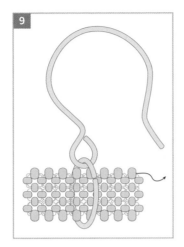

Stitch help: To work around the jump ring, you may sometimes want to pass the needle and thread through it before beginning a new stitch. If you're careful, you can also shimmy the jump ring down to the already-zipped section and out of your path.

15 Continue zipping up the tube. Add 1 yellow, 1 turquoise, 1 yellow, 1 turquoise, 1 black rice drop, 1 turquoise, 1 white rice drop, 1 turquoise, 1 yellow, 1 turquoise, 1 white rice drop, 1 turquoise, and 1 more black rice drop.

16 Alternate turquoise and yellow beads along the center around the edge to complete the earring, working carefully around the jump ring. After adding the final size 11 bead in the pattern, weave around 4 size 11 beads to join the first and last beads added and complete the RAW cluster and close the ring. Secure any remaining thread and trim.

17 Repeat all steps to make a second earring. Adjust the position of the jump ring if necessary, so that the drop beads are centered at the bottom.

10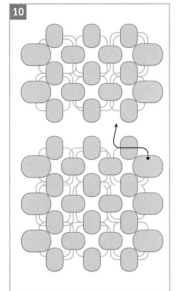

11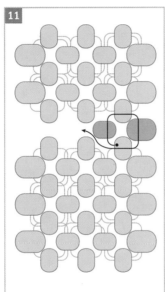

12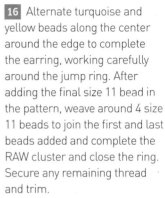

13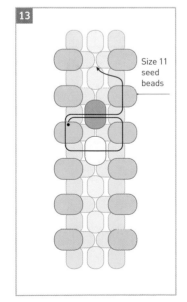

Size 11 seed beads

15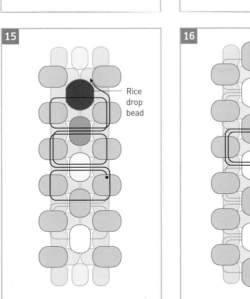

Rice drop bead

16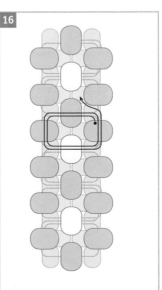

Choosing beads: Size 11 Czech seed beads create the best shape for this project, though you can use any brand of size 15 that you like. Switch to your size 13 beading needle if you encounter any tight spaces in the beadwork, particularly in the size 15 bead sections.

Jeweled Collar

The combination of Aurora Borealis and Picasso bead finishes in this piece give it a mysterious look, like an uncut gemstone. Inspired by the classic combination of gold, lapis, and carnelian—used in many Egyptian artworks, such as the decorated sarcophagus, left—this necklace will make a stunning jewel in your collection. Although double chevron chain can be worked by stitching a new chain directly onto the first, the addition of two-hole beads gives an extra element of drama to this piece.

SKILL LEVEL: **INTERMEDIATE**
TECHNIQUE: **CHEVRON CHAIN**

TOOLS AND MATERIALS

- 12 yd (11 m) smoke braided beading line, 6 lb test (size D)
- Size 10 beading needle

Beads

- 25 g matte black AB 11/0 seed beads (1)
- 5 g light topaz AB 11/0 seed beads (2)
- 52 x 3 mm coral Picasso two-hole tube beads (3)
- 51 x 2 mm coral Picasso uno drops (3)

Dimensions: 1¼ x 21 in. (3 x 54 cm)

COLOR PALETTE

| 1 | 2 | 3 |

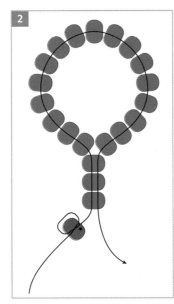

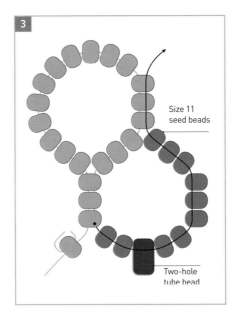

Size 11 seed beads

Two-hole tube bead

1 Combine the matte black and topaz seed beads and mix thoroughly to blend the colors. Thread a needle with 1 yd (0.9 m) of beading line, and create a toggle clasp that is 12 beads long with a picot trim, choosing the colors at random (Techniques, page 134). Set the clasp aside.

2 Thread a needle with 2 yd (1.8 m) of beading line and attach a stop bead with a 10-in. (25-cm) tail. Pick up 20 seed beads. Slide them down to the stop bead, and stitch back through the first 3 seed beads picked up.

3 Pick up 2 seed beads, 1 tube bead, and 8 seed beads. Stitch up through the 15th, 16th, and 17th beads added in the previous step (or 6 beads up from the place your thread is exiting).

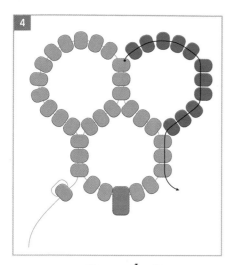

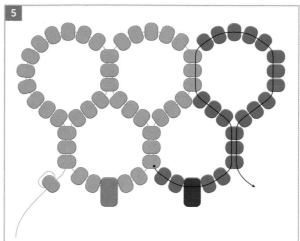

Stitch help: The two-hole beads create a stiff core to the double chevron chain that would hinder the drape of a full-length collar. The chain clasp technique is not only a great way to make an authentic-looking Egyptian necklace, it can also save a collar design that has too much curve. It's a great technique to have in your repertoire.

4 Pick up 11 seed beads and stitch down through the third, fourth, and fifth beads added in the previous step.

5 Repeat steps 3 and 4 until you have added all 52 tube beads, adding new thread as needed. Finish the net with an 11 seed bead stitch (step 4), then weave back through the last stitch again.

6 Pick up 67 seed beads and stitch back through the 29th bead added again. Pick up 3 seed beads. Skipping 3 beads in the strand, stitch through the following bead, and pull snug. Repeat along the entire strand.

7 Weave into the chevron chain, and back around into the clasp chain. Weave any remaining thread into the clasp chain and trim.

8 Remove the stop bead from the first thread. Weave around the first stitch, and exit from the start point again. Pick up 36 seed beads, then pass through 2 center beads of the peyote toggle.

9 Pick up 3 seed beads. Skipping 3 in the strand, pass through the following bead and pull snug. Repeat along the entire strand. Weave any remaining thread into the clasp chain and trim.

10 Attach a stop bead to 2 yd (1.8 m) of beading line, leaving a 10-in. (25-cm) tail. Pick up 11 seed beads, and pass through the second hole of the first tube bead added in the previous chain.

11 Pick up 8 seed beads, and stitch down through the first 3 beads added in the previous step.

12 Pick up 3 seed beads, 1 uno drop, and 9 seed beads. Stitch up through the third, fourth, and fifth beads added in the previous step.

13 Pick up 2 seed beads, and pass through the second hole of the next tube bead in the chain. Pick up 8 seed beads, and stitch down through the fourth, fifth, and sixth beads added in the previous step.

14 Repeat steps 9 and 10 until you've added all 51 uno drop beads. Finish with an 8 seed bead stitch (step 11). Weave in any remaining threads and trim.

Play with patterns: The unique structure of the netting provides plenty of opportunity to play with color and pattern. Any section of the chevron chain can be blocked from the others with a change in color, to create pleasing shapes within the beadwork.

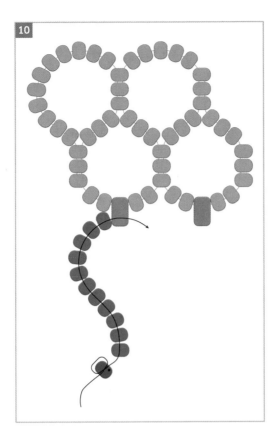

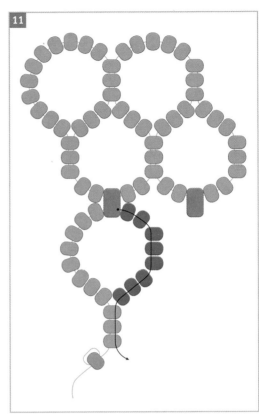

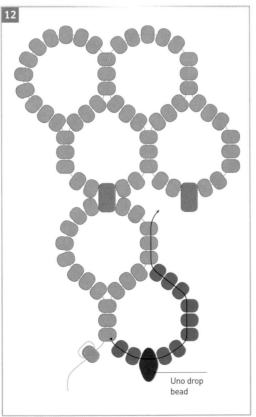

Uno drop bead

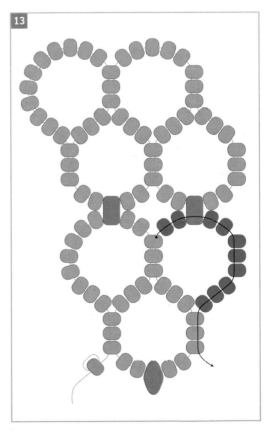

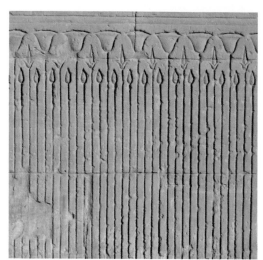

Reed Cuff

The Ancient Egyptians used papyrus reeds to create everyday objects such as boats, footwear, and mats. This bracelet draws inspiration from woven mats and traditional stripe patterns, such as the lotus carvings at the Temple of Horus, seen left. Bugle beads are an excellent choice for adding bold stripe patterns and geometric elements to beadwork. Some bugles can have sharp edges that cut threads, so in this bracelet the stitches are protected by extra seed beads that also help to fill in the rows with a pretty stripe pattern.

SKILL LEVEL: INTERMEDIATE
TECHNIQUES: SQUARE STITCH,
MODIFIED BRICK STITCH

TOOLS AND MATERIALS

- 20 yd (18 m) black braided beading line, 6 lb test (size D)
- Size 10 beading needle

Beads
- 8 g opaque black 11/0 Japanese seed beads (1)
- 8 g bone white 11/0 Japanese seed beads (2)
- 10 g brown satin 6 mm bugle beads (3)

Dimensions: 1½ x 6 in. (4 x 15 cm)

COLOR PALETTE

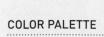

1 Thread a needle with 1 yd (0.9 m) of beading line. Using black seed beads, create a peyote toggle 12 beads long, with a bone white trim (Techniques, page 134). Set aside.

2 Attach a stop bead to a 2-yd (1.8-m) length of beading line, leaving a 12-in. (30-cm) tail. Pick up 1 bone, 1 bugle, 4 bone, 1 bugle, 4 bone, 1 bugle, and 1 bone seed bead. Slide them down to the end, and turn the thread so that the stop bead faces away from you.

3 Pick up 1 bone, 1 bugle, and 1 black seed bead. Stitch down through the last 3 beads of the previous row (1 bone, 1 bugle, 1 bone). Pull snug so that the new beads line up, then stitch up through all three beads just added to form the first square stitch section.

4 Pick up 2 black seed beads. Stitch down through the adjacent 2 bone beads in the previous row. Pull snug, and stitch up through the 2 beads just added.

5 Pick up 1 black, 1 bugle, and 1 black seed bead. Stitch down through the 3 adjacent beads of the previous row. Pull snug, and stitch up through the 3 new beads.

6 Add 2 black seed beads as before with square stitch (step 4), followed by 1 black, 1 bugle, and 1 bone seed bead. Turn the beadwork to begin the next row.

7 Repeat steps 3 to 6, adding new thread as needed, until the beadwork is 5½ in. (14 cm) long, or about ¾ in. (2 cm) short of your desired bracelet length. Alternate from bone to black seed beads for the center rows only, leaving the edges white.

8 Stitch down through the previous row, then turn to exit from a seed bead next to the center-most bugle. Pick up 26 black seed beads.

Stitch help: Always choose the nearest available bridge thread when adding the picot trim, and try to keep the area of beadwork you are stitching flat, to prevent puckering.

Bead selection: When choosing bugle beads, watch out for slanted or broken edges. Though the seed bead bumpers in the bugle rows will protect your thread, flat-edged bugles will give a more uniform appearance to your bracelet.

2-3

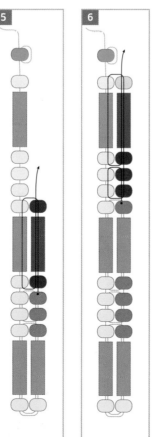

4

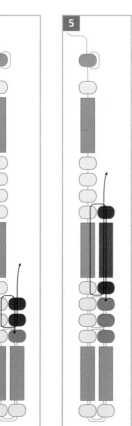

5

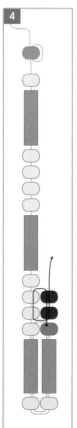

6

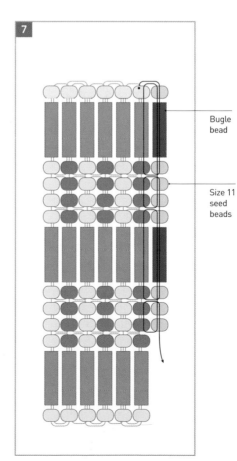

7

Bugle bead

Size 11 seed beads

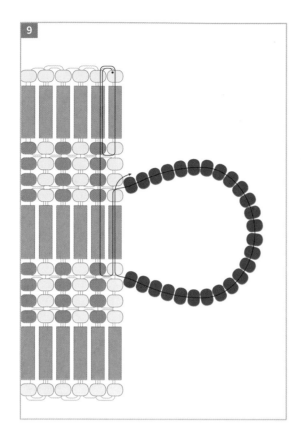

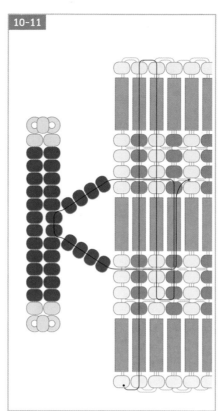

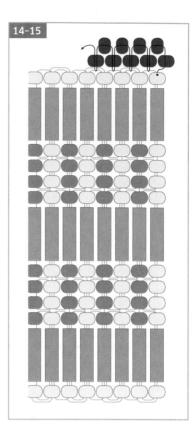

9 Stitch through the seed bead on the opposite side of the center bugle. Test the fit of the loop against the clasp toggle, and add or remove beads as needed. Weave through the loop twice, then secure any remaining thread in the beadwork and trim.

10 Remove the stop bead from the original tail thread. Weave through the beadwork to exit from the center of the fourth row.

11 Pick up 4 black seed beads and pass through the center 2 beads of the toggle. Add 4 black, and pass through the opposite seed bead in the center of the row.

12 Weave through the toggle section twice, then secure any remaining thread and trim. Weave in any remaining tail threads.

13 Attach a stop bead to 2 yd (1.8 m) of thread, leaving a 6-in. (15-cm) tail. Weave into the beadwork, and exit from a corner seed bead on the edge.

14 Pick up 3 black seed beads. Pass the needle under the nearest bridge of thread between beads, moving toward you. Pull snug, and stitch up through the last bead added to form a picot.

15 Pick up 2 black seed beads. Pass under the nearest bridge. Pull snug and stitch up through the second bead just added. Repeat along the edge of the cuff.

16 Add the last picot, covering the final row of the cuff. Pass through the rows at the edge to exit from the opposite edge. Repeat steps 14 and 15 to add the picot trim to this side. Weave in remaining thread and trim.

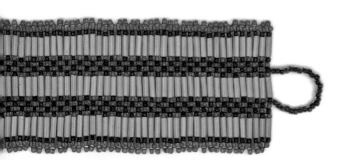

The bold shape of the bugles in this cuff create stunning stripes in any palette.

Lotus Earrings

Representing renewal and the arrival of a new day, lotus blossoms and motifs were common in Ancient Egyptian art and architecture, as seen in the papyrus painting, left. The simple petal shapes are mimicked in these earrings by daggers and drops of varying sizes, with a soft palette of aquatic blues and browns. Braided beading line is used in these earrings to give the fringe loops a more uniform shape, while the antique copper findings add an ancient flair.

SKILL LEVEL: INTERMEDIATE
TECHNIQUES: BRICK STITCH, STRINGING

TOOLS AND MATERIALS

- 2 x 18-gauge (1-mm) 6 mm antique copper-plated jump rings
- 2 x 18-gauge (1-mm) antique copper-plated earwires
- 2¾ yd (2.5 m) black braided beading line, 6 lb test (size D)
- Size 10 beading needle

Beads
- 4 g matte cobalt blue 11/0 seed beads (1)
- 2 g opaque turquoise 11/0 seed beads (2)
- 12 x 4 mm natural bone round beads (3)
- 24 opaque turquoise 8/0 seed beads (2)
- 8 x 3.5 mm beige Picasso fringe drops (4)
- 4 x 2 mm brown Picasso uno drops (5)
- 4 x 2.5 mm green Picasso rice drops (6)
- 2 x 20 mm Capri blue glass daggers (7)

Dimensions: 3¼ x 1 in. (8 x 2.5 cm)

COLOR PALETTE

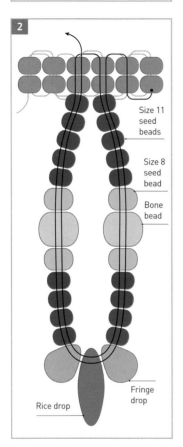

Size 11
seed
beads

Size 8
seed
bead

Bone
bead

Rice drop

Fringe
drop

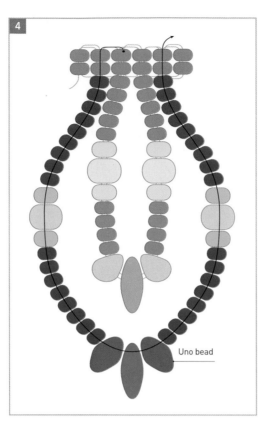

Uno bead

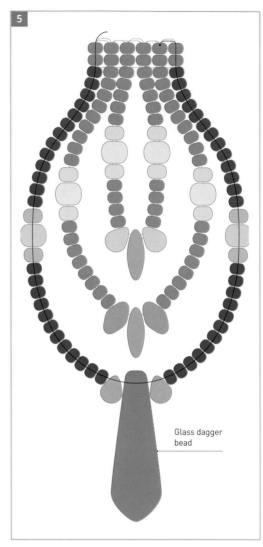

Glass dagger
bead

Bead selection: The bone beads help reduce the weight of these bold earrings, which might otherwise be quite bulky. For an even lighter variation, use smaller dagger beads, or replace them with drops of your choice.

1 Thread a needle on a 50-in. (1.2-m) length of beading line. Using size 11 cobalt blue beads, stitch a 2-bead ladder that is 6 columns wide, leaving a 6-in. (15-cm) tail (Techniques, page 132).

2 Weave through the beads to exit from the bottom of the fourth column. Pick up 5 blue size 11 beads, 1 size 8 bead, 1 bone bead, 1 size 8 bead, 4 blue size 11 beads, and 1 fringe drop. Add 1 rice drop, then repeat the pattern in reverse.

3 Stitch up through the third column of the bead ladder, and pull snug. Stitch back down through the fourth column, and pass through all of the beads just added, exiting from the drop of the ladder.

4 Stitch down through the second column of the ladder. Pick up 9 blue size 11 beads, 1 size 8 bead, 1 bone bead, 1 size 8 bead, 8 blue size 11 beads, and 1 uno bead. Add 1 rice drop, then repeat the pattern in reverse.

5 Stitch up through the fifth column of the bead ladder, then down through the sixth. Pick up 13 blue size 11 beads, 1 size 8 bead, 1 bone bead, 1 size 8 bead, 12 blue size 11 beads, and 1 drop bead. Add a dagger, and repeat the pattern in reverse.

6 Stitch up through the first column of the bead ladder. Stitch down through the second column, and pass through the middle loop. Stitch down through the sixth column, and pass through the outside loop. Exit from the top of the bead

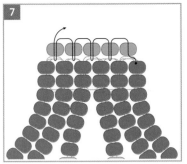

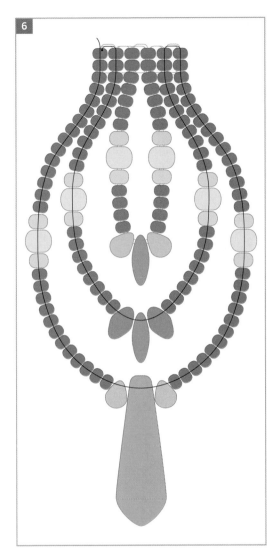

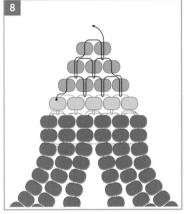

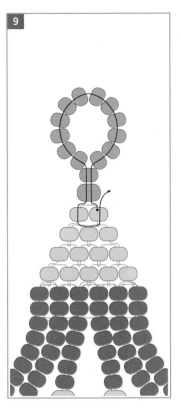

ladder, and turn the beadwork so the thread is on the right.

7 Pick up 2 turquoise size 11 beads. Skipping the first bridge of thread in the ladder, bring the thread under the next bridge, and pull snug. Stitch up through the second bead just added. Add 3 more turquoise size 11 beads, one at a time, with this brick stitch method.

8 Repeat step 7 to add 4 seed beads to the next row with brick stitch. Add a row of 3 seed beads and a final row of 2 seed beads.

9 Pick up 1 size 8 bead and 13 turquoise size 11 beads. Stitch down through the first size 11 just added and the size 8. Pass through the second seed bead in the top row of brick stitch—opposite the bead your thread is exiting.

10 Stitch up through the opposite bead in the top row, and pass through the loop. Repeat, then secure all remaining thread and trim.

11 Open a jump ring. Thread on an earwire and the top earring loop. Close the jump ring. Repeat all steps to make a second earring.

Valley of the Queens Cuff

Named for the resting place of Egypt's royal ladies—such as Neferari, shown left—this bracelet is inspired by anklets once worn by an Egyptian princess. The beaded bands were made from colorful beads strung between wide gold spacers, and featured beautiful cloisonné charms. In this variation, drop beads add movement to a sturdy but flexible cuff. Square stitch stands in for the metal spacers in this design. To cut down on tail threads and restarts, the base is woven in one continuous motion, then filled in with additional strands of beads. Overall, the pattern provides a lot of opportunity to play with classic Egyptian stripes and rectangular motifs. For a more challenging variation of the technique, try the Papyrus Collar on page 42.

SKILL LEVEL: **INTERMEDIATE**
TECHNIQUE: **MODIFIED SQUARE STITCH**

TOOLS AND MATERIALS

- 12 yd (11 m) smoke braided beading line, 6 lb test (size D)
- Size 10 beading needle

Beads
- 12 g transparent cobalt 11/0 seed beads (1)
- 3 g opaque black 11/0 seed beads (2)
- 3 g buttercream 11/0 Ceylon seed beads (3)
- 4 x 6 mm opalescent aqua fringe drops (4)

Dimensions: 1½ x 7 in. (4 x 18 cm)

COLOR PALETTE

1	2
3	4

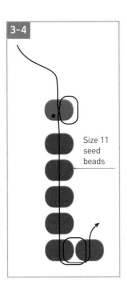

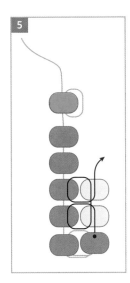

Size 11 seed beads

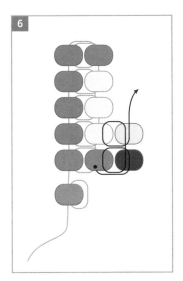

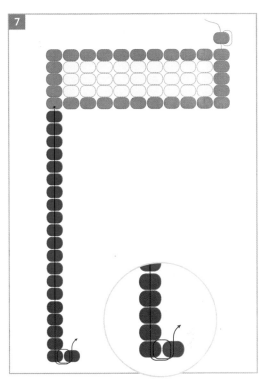

1 Thread a needle with 1 yd (0.9 m) of beading line, and create a peyote bead toggle 12 beads long in black, with a buttercream trim (Techniques, page 134). Set aside.

2 Thread a needle on a 2-yd (1.5-m) length of beading line. Attach a stop bead, leaving an 8-in. (20-cm) tail.

3 Pick up 5 black seed beads, and slide them down to the stop bead. Turn the thread so that the tail thread is pointing away from you.

4 Pick up 1 black seed bead and stitch down through the fifth seed bead just added. Stitch up through the new bead, and pull snug to form the first square stitch.

5 Pick up 1 buttercream seed bead and stitch down through the next black seed bead in the previous row, then up through the new bead just added. Repeat to add 2 more buttercream seed beads and 1 black seed bead. Flip the beadwork so that the bead just added is pointing toward you.

6 Repeat step 5 to add more rows with square stitch. Add 8 rows with 3 buttercream seed beads at the center and a final row in all black seed beads for a panel that is 11 rows wide.

7 After passing through the final seed bead in the end row, pick up 15 cobalt blue seed beads and 5 black seed beads. Pushing the new beads up to the first panel, pick up 1 black seed bead, and connect it to the fifth seed bead just added using square stitch, to start the next panel.

8 Finish the panel with square stitch, using the same pattern of black and buttercream seed beads. Pick up 15 cobalt and 5 black seed beads, then add a third square stitch panel.

9 Pick up 5 cobalt seed beads, 1 drop, 3 cobalt, 1 drop, 5 cobalt, and 5 black seed beads. Add a new square stitch panel, then repeat to add a second set of drops.

Variations: Try experimenting with different types or sizes of drops to change the look of your bracelet. Your sections will also change dramatically by adding vertical or horizontal stripe patterns in a few different colors.

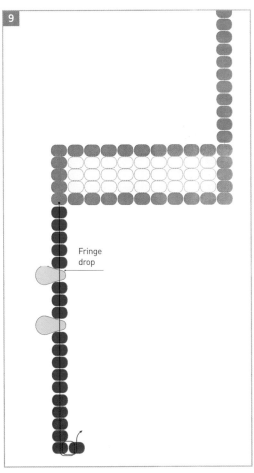

Fringe drop

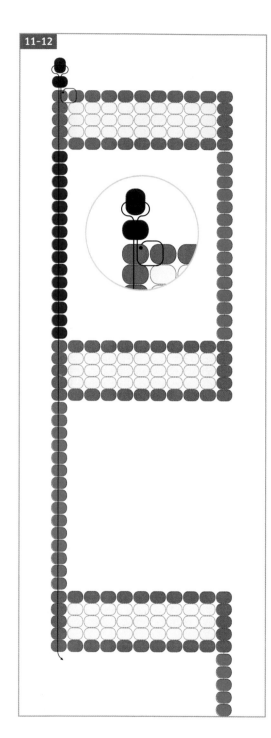

11-12

14-15

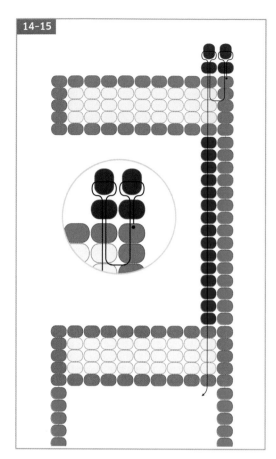

10 Continue weaving, adding 3 more square stitch panels with 15 cobalt beads between them, for a total of 7 square stitch panels. Add new thread as needed, being sure to weave your new threads in the same direction.

11 Stitch through the last bead added to complete the final panel. Pick up 2 black beads. Skipping the second bead, stitch back through the first black seed bead added and the 5 black seed beads at the edge of the panel.

12 Pick up 15 cobalt seed beads and stitch through the last row of the following panel. Pass through the 15 cobalt seed beads already added and the following panel.

13 Pick up 5 cobalt, 1 drop, 3 cobalt, 1 drop, and 5 cobalt seed beads. Pass through the next panel, the existing cobalt and drop beads, and the following panel. Add 15 cobalt beads to the next gap, and pass through all remaining beads to exit the last panel.

14 Pick up 2 black seed beads. Skipping the second bead, stitch through the first bead and the next 2 beads in the square stitch panel. Stitch up through the top 2 beads of the next row in the panel.

15 Pick up 2 black seed beads, and stitch back through the first bead added and the following 5 beads in the panel. Pick up 15 cobalt seed beads, and stitch through the following panel.

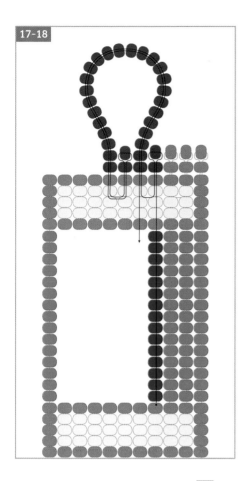

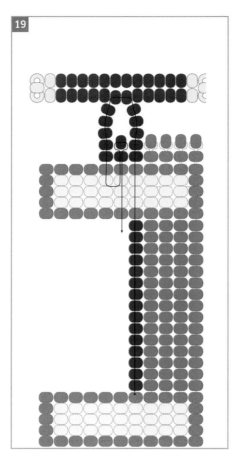

Repeat to fill all the gaps, and exit from the opposite edge of the beadwork.

16 Add a 2-bead fringe, and turn as before. Add a 2-bead fringe to the next row, and continue adding 15 cobalt beads to each gap for the rest of the row.

17 Exit from the opposite edge, add a 2-bead fringe, and turn to exit the next row. Pick up 26 black seed beads. Skipping 1 row in the panel, stitch down through the next row to form a loop.

18 Stitch up through the row that was skipped, and add a 2-bead fringe. Pass through the panel and up into the clasp loop. Exit from the panel to start the next row. Fill in all gaps with 15 cobalt seed beads.

19 Exit from the panel at the opposite edge, and pick up 5 black seed beads. Pass through two beads at the center of the beaded toggle, and pick up 5 black seed beads. Skipping 1 row in the panel, stitch down through the next row.

20 Stitch up through the skipped row in the panel. Add a 2-bead fringe, pass through the panel, and add 15 cobalt seed beads. Fill in all gaps in this row.

21 At the loop edge, stitch up through the first 3 beads in the panel, then up through 2 in the next row in the panel. Pass through the clasp loop to exit the next row and fill with cobalt.

22 At the toggle edge, stitch up through the first 3 beads of the panel and up through 2 beads in the next. Add a 2-bead fringe to turn, and fill in the gaps of the next 3 rows, turning as usual.

23 Add a 2-bead fringe to the final row. Pass through the cobalt seed beads already added and the following panel. Add 15 cobalt seed beads to the next gap.

24 In the following gap, add 5 cobalt, 1 drop, 3 cobalt, 1 drop, and 5 cobalt seed beads. Pass through the panel and following strand. Add 15 cobalt seed beads to the final gap and a 2-bead fringe at the end of the row.

25 Weave in all remaining thread and tails, passing through the toggle area twice with the original tail thread.

Nubian Collar

This necklace is inspired by an ancient collar from Nubia, the Egyptians' favorite source for gold, which was used in everything from jewelry to artworks like the papyrus seen here. The organic shapes of the accent beads used in this design create a very ancient-looking collar. Though it looks elaborate, the stitches are deceptively simple to weave.

SKILL LEVEL: INTERMEDIATE
TECHNIQUE: NETTING

TOOLS AND MATERIALS

- 20 yd (18 m) smoke braided beading line, 6 lb test (Size D)
- Size 10 beading needle

Beads
- 150 large (4–5 mm) African Christmas beads (1)
- 76 x 4 mm wood tube beads (2)
- 152 blue-and-red striped 8/0 seed beads (3)
- 300 opaque black 8/0 seed beads (4)
- 75 canary yellow 8/0 seed beads (5)
- 46 x 4 mm cobalt blue glass drops (6)
- 28 x 8 mm large-hole cobalt blue glass drops (6)
- 60 g opaque black 11/0 seed beads (4)
- 1 x 26 mm blue iris Czech glass button (7)

Dimensions: 2½ x 20 in. (6.5 x 50 cm)

COLOR PALETTE

1 Gently wash your Christmas beads with plain warm water, and allow to dry overnight. If desired, count out 150 similarly shaped beads before you begin, or choose as you work.

2 Thread a needle with 2 yd (1.8 m) of beading line, and attach a stop bead, leaving a tail of 12 in. (30 cm). String 1 yellow size 8, 5 black size 11, 1 wood tube, 5 black size 11, 1 black size 8, 2 black size 11, 1 black size 8, 2 Christmas beads, 1 black size 8, 2 black size 11, 1 black size 8, 4 black size 11, 1 striped size 8, 4 black size 11, 1 striped size 8, and 8 black size 11 seed beads.

3 Stitch back through the seventh black seed bead just added and pull snug.

4 Pick up 6 black size 11 beads, and pass down through the topmost striped size 8 bead.

5 Pick up 4 black size 11, 1 striped size 8, and 4 black size 11 beads. Pass down through the topmost black size 8 bead from the previous row and continue through the following 9 beads, to exit from the lowest black size 8 bead.

6 Pick up 5 black size 11, 1 wood tube, and 5 black size 11. Pass down through the yellow size 8 bead from the previous row.

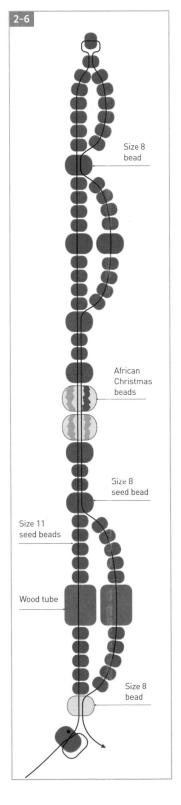

2-6

Size 8 bead

African Christmas beads

Size 8 seed bead

Size 11 seed beads

Wood tube

Size 8 bead

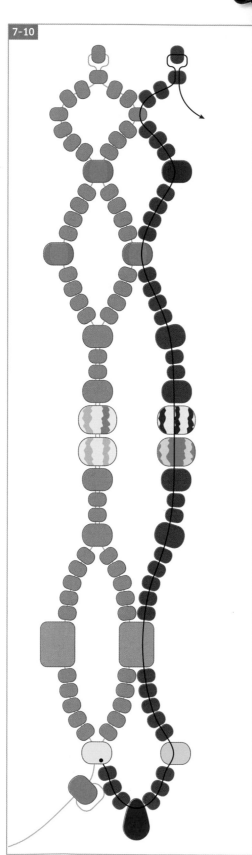

7 Pick up 3 black size 11, 1 blue 4 mm drop, 3 black size 11, 1 yellow size 8, and 5 black size 11. Stitch up through the wood tube just added, and pull snug.

8 Pick up 5 black size 11, 1 black size 8, 2 black size 11, 1 black size 8, 2 Christmas beads, 1 black size 8, 2 black size 11, 1 black size 8, and 4 black size 11 beads. Stitch up through the lower striped size 8 from the previous row.

9 Pick up 4 black size 11, 1 striped size 8, and 3 black size 11. Stitch up through the fourth black size 11 bead in the previous row.

10 Add 4 black size 11 beads, and stitch back down through the third bead added.

11 Repeat steps 4 to 10, adding new thread as needed, until you have a net with 23 blue drops along the bottom edge.

12 Continue weaving in the same pattern, adding an additional black size 11 bead and a blue 8 mm drop bead in place of the smaller drops. The seed beads should pass easily through the drop holes. Add 28 blue 8 mm drops, then return to the original pattern to add the remaining 23 blue 4 mm drops.

Bead selection: The large glass drops add a lot of weight to an already bold necklace. If you prefer a more understated look, use smaller drops all along the edge. Include all one color, or alternate colors in a pleasing pattern.

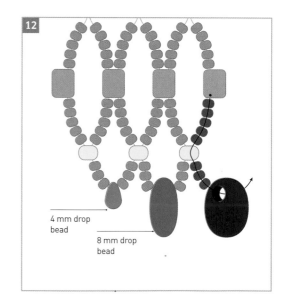

4 mm drop bead

8 mm drop bead

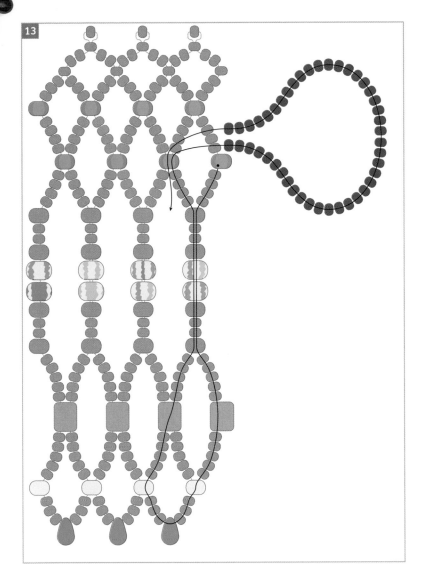

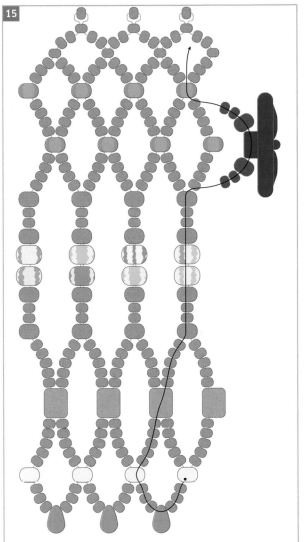

13 Finish the net with a downward row, then weave through the beadwork to exit from the lower striped bead of the previous row. Pick up 40 to 45 black size 11 beads, and pass through the striped bead again to form a loop. Test the fit of the loop on your button, and add or remove beads if necessary.

14 Pass through the final rows of the net and through the clasp loop again twice to secure it. Secure any remaining thread in the beadwork and trim.

15 Remove the stop bead from the start of the beadwork, and thread a needle on the tail. Weave around the edge to exit up through the topmost black size 8 bead of the second row.

16 Pick up 2 black size 11, 1 black size 8, the button shank, 1 black size 8, and 2 black size 11 beads. Stitch up through the topmost striped bead of the row. Weave around the beadwork edge and through the button section twice more, then secure all remaining thread and trim.

Project planning: African Christmas beads, or love beads, can vary greatly in size and shape. You'll need about four 22-in. (56-cm) strands to work from, so that you can choose the best beads for your project. If you're not able to find genuine trade beads, size 6 seed beads or 4 mm round beads in opaque colors will work just as well.

TOOLS AND MATERIALS

- 44 yd (40 m) smoke braided beading line, 6 lb test (size D)
- Size 10 beading needle

Beads

- 50 g opaque black 11/0 Czech seed beads (1)
- 40 g transparent Montana blue 11/0 Czech seed beads (2)
- 20 g matte blue 11/0 Japanese seed beads (3)
- 10 g transparent topaz 11/0 Japanese seed beads (4)
- 12 x 2.5 mm black rice drop beads (1)
- 5 x 16 mm black glass dagger beads (1)

Dimensions: 1¾ x 16 in. (4.5 x 40 cm)

COLOR PALETTE

1	2	3	4

Papyrus Collar

The papyrus reeds that grew along the Nile were incredibly important in day-to-day life in Ancient Egypt. Among its other uses, the world's first-known writing material was made by layering strips of papyrus reeds at right angles to form sheets of fibrous paper (see left). This necklace draws inspiration from the overlapping strips of papyrus, which is still used today in artwork sold to tourists in Egypt. It is an expanded version of the Valley of the Queens Cuff on page 34, with a slight change in bead quantities to create a perfectly draped collar.

1 Thread a needle with 1 yd (0.9 m) of beading line. Using topaz seed beads, create a peyote toggle 12 beads long, with a trim of size 11 black beads (Techniques, page 134). Set aside.

2 Attach a stop bead to 2 yd (1.8 m) of beading line, leaving a 10-in. (25-cm) tail. Pick up 2 matte blue seed beads, 2 topaz, and 2 matte blue. Slide them down the thread, with the stop bead facing away from you.

3 Pick up 1 matte blue seed bead, and stitch down through the last bead added. Stitch up through the new bead and pull snug.

4 Pick up 1 matte blue seed bead, and stitch down through the next bead in the previous row. Stitch up through the new bead, and pull snug. Repeat for 2 topaz and 2 matte blue to finish the row with this square stitch method.

5 Turn the beadwork to begin the next row. Add 2 matte blue, 2 topaz, and 2 matte blue beads with square stitch. Repeat until you have a strip that is 17 beads wide.

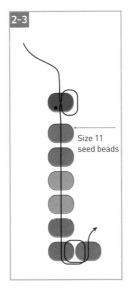

Size 11 seed beads

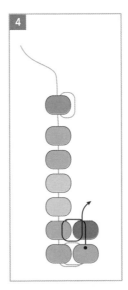

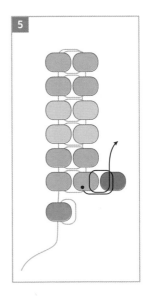

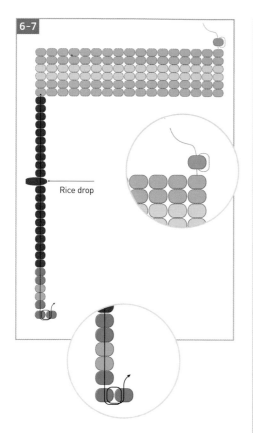

Rice drop

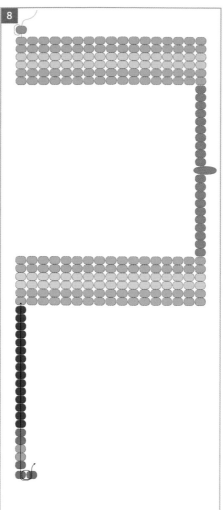

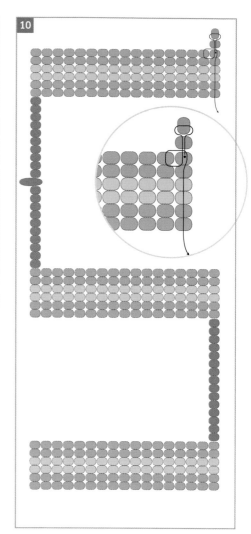

6 Pick up 10 size 11 black beads, 1 rice drop, and 10 size 11 black beads. Add 2 matte blue, 2 topaz, and 2 matte blue seed beads. With the previous square stitch panel facing away from you, push the new beads up securely.

7 Add 1 matte blue seed bead with square stitch to begin a new panel, making sure that there is no slack thread in the strand of black seed beads. Complete the row, and add 15 more square stitch rows in the same pattern to create a second panel.

8 Pick up 15 Montana blue seed beads, 2 matte blue, 2 topaz, and 2 matte blue. Slide them up and add 16 rows of

square stitch to make a third panel.

9 Repeat steps 6 to 8, alternating between additions of Montana blue and black seed beads between each panel. In the black sections, add 2 more rice drops, followed by 3 dagger beads, then 3 more rice drops.

10 Add a final panel to the beadwork, for a total of 18 square stitch panels. Stitch up through the last bead added to complete the panel and pick up 2 topaz seed beads.

11 Stitch down through the first bead just added, and pass through all 6 beads in the last row of square stitch.

12 Pick up 15 Montana blue beads, and pass through the last row of the next square stitch panel. Continue through the following 15 Montana blue beads and the next panel. Repeat until you reach the first square stitch panel to fill in all of the gaps, and exit from the edge.

13 Pick up 2 topaz beads. Stitch back through the first bead added and the top 4 beads

in the square stitch panel. Stitch up through the top 4 beads in the next row to exit the edge again.

14 Add a 2-bead fringe with topaz seed beads and pass through all 6 beads in the square stitch row. Pick up 15 Montana blue beads, and pass through the second row in the following panel. Repeat for the entire length of the beadwork, exiting from the end panel.

15 Repeat step 13, adding 2 topaz fringes and turning to start the next set of strands.

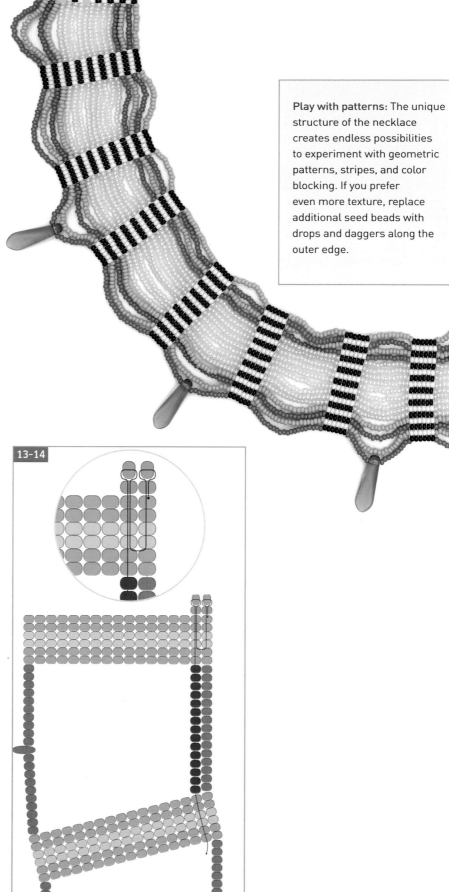

12

Play with patterns: The unique structure of the necklace creates endless possibilities to experiment with geometric patterns, stripes, and color blocking. If you prefer even more texture, replace additional seed beads with drops and daggers along the outer edge.

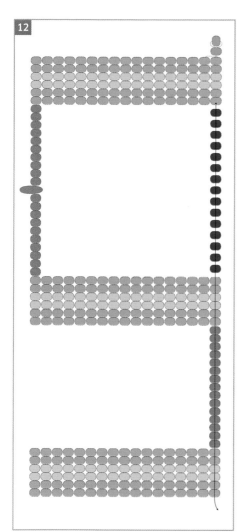

13-14

Stitch help: Once the first few rows are filled, the shape of the collar is set. If you find that your bead strands appear too short, it is safe to add one or two more seed beads to each gap. The irregular lengths of the Czech seed beads add to the ancient quality of the necklace, so when in doubt, add more rather than less.

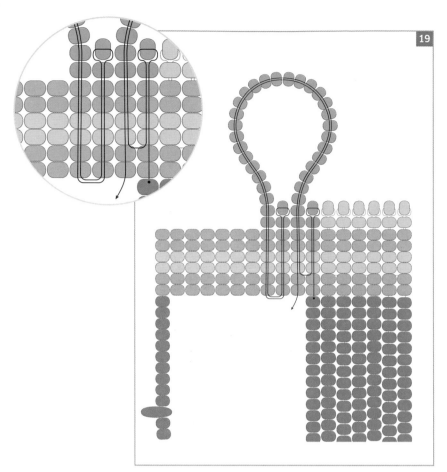

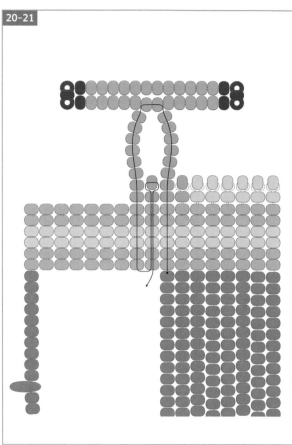

16 Add 16 Montana blue seed beads to each gap for 3 rows, adding fringe and turning at the end of each row.

17 Add 17 Montana blue seed beads to each gap for 2 rows. At the end of the second row, add a 2-bead fringe, and turn to exit the edge of the panel. Pick up 35 to 40 topaz seed beads. Skipping 1 row in the panel, stitch down through the next row and pull snug to form a clasp loop. Test the fit of the loop on your peyote toggle, and add or remove beads if necessary.

18 Stitch up through the center square stitch row that was skipped. Add a 2-bead fringe with topaz seed beads, and stitch down through all 6 beads in the row.

19 Stitch up through the far side of the loop and down through the panel to start the next row. Add 17 Montana blue beads per gap, and exit from the edge of the last panel.

20 Pick up 8 topaz beads, and pass through 2 beads at the center of the peyote toggle. Add 8 topaz beads. Skipping 1 square stitch row, stitch down through the next row in the panel.

21 Stitch up through the center row, add a 2-bead fringe, and pass through all 6 beads of the panel.

22 Add 18 size 11 black beads per gap for the entire row. Pass through the first 4 beads of the last square stitch panel and up through the top 2 of the previous row. Pass through the clasp loop to exit the next row.

23 Add 2 rows with 18 size 11 black beads in each gap, turning and adding fringe as before. Add 3 rows with 19 size 11 black beads, followed by 2 rows with 20 size 11 black beads per gap.

24 Add fringe, and turn at the end of the final row. Pass through the size 11 black beads and rice drop in the first gap and the following square stitch panel.

25 Add 10 size 11 black seed beads, 1 rice drop, and 10 size 11 black beads for the next 3 gaps, passing through the previously added beads as necessary.

26 Add 10 black seed beads, 1 dagger, and 10 black seed beads for the next 2 gaps. Finish the row, adding 1 rice drop to the remaining 3 sections.

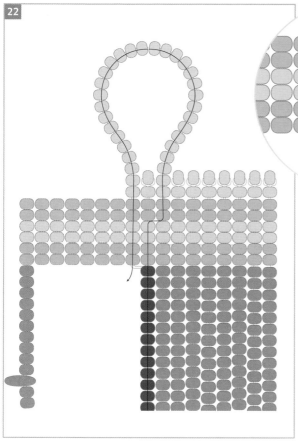

27 Add a 2-bead fringe to the final row of the edge panel. Weave in all remaining threads and trim.

Pharaoh Collar

Few Ancient Egyptian monarchs are more recognizable than the boy king Tutankhamun. The face of his funerary mask (seen left) is an icon of the Ancient Egyptian civilization for the modern world. This necklace draws inspiration from the beautiful collar engraved on the mask in traditional colors of turquoise, lapis, and carnelian. This collar uses a very basic netting design found in tribal beadwork around the world. There is only a gradual increase in stitch sizes to create the curve, which is enhanced by gathering the inner edge together.

SKILL LEVEL: ADVANCED
TECHNIQUE: NETTING

TOOLS AND MATERIALS

- 22 yd (20 m) smoke braided beading line, 6 lb test (size D)
- Size 10 beading needle

Beads
- 25 g transparent ruby iris 11/0 Czech seed beads [1]
- 25 g transparent cobalt blue 11/0 Czech seed beads [2]
- 15 g transparent light topaz 11/0 Czech seed beads [3]
- 15 g turquoise iris 11/0 Czech seed beads [4]
- 1 x 6 mm ruby AB glass druk bead [1]

Dimensions: 1½ x 16 in. (4 x 41 cm)

COLOR PALETTE

1	2	3	4

1 With 1 yd (0.9 m) of beading line, create a brick stitch button using your druk bead (Techniques, page 137), alternating bead colors for 3 rows. Add a row of picots to the edge (Techniques, page 138) and set aside.

2 Thread a needle with 2 yd (1.8 m) of beading line and attach a stop bead, leaving a 10-in. (25-cm) tail.

3 String 1 topaz, 5 cobalt, 1 topaz, 5 turquoise, 1 topaz, 5 cobalt, 1 topaz, 5 ruby, 1 topaz, 3 cobalt, and 1 topaz bead. Skipping the last topaz bead just added, stitch down through the next 4 beads, exiting from the second topaz bead just added.

4 Pick up 5 ruby seed beads and stitch down through the next topaz bead in the previous row. Repeat, adding 5 cobalt, 5 turquoise, and 5 cobalt beads, and exiting from the first topaz picked up.

5 Pick up 3 ruby and 2 topaz beads. Skipping the last topaz bead, stitch up through the first topaz added, and pull snug.

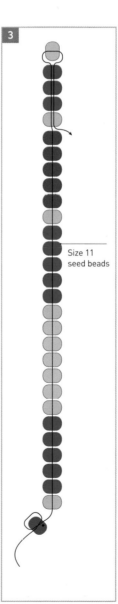

Size 11 seed beads

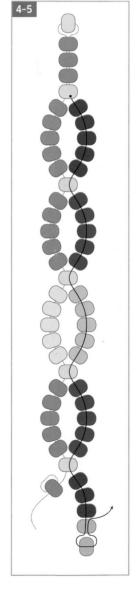

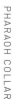

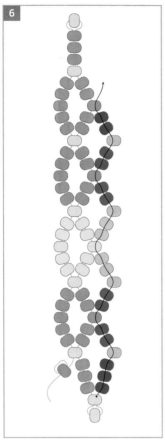

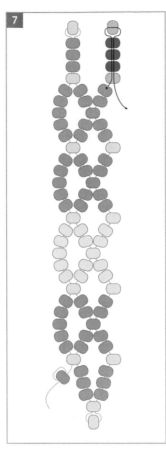

6 Pick up 3 ruby, 1 topaz, and 2 cobalt beads. Stitch up through the middle cobalt of the previous row. Repeat this step, stitching through the center bead of each color block for each new set of 5 beads. Add 2 cobalt, 1 topaz, 2 turquoise; 2 turquoise, 1 topaz, 2 cobalt; 2 cobalt, 1 topaz, and 2 ruby.

7 Pick up 2 ruby, 1 topaz, 3 cobalt, and 1 topaz bead. Skipping the topaz bead just added, stitch down through the next 4 beads, exiting from the next topaz of the row.

8 Repeat steps 3 to 6, adding new thread as needed, until you have a net that is about 20 in. (50 cm) in length. Finish with a downward row.

9 Weave through the edge of the net, and exit from the lower 2 beads of the ruby block, 4 rows in from the edge.

10 Pick up 4 ruby beads, pass through the druk bead of your button, and add 4 ruby beads. Stitch up through the top 2 cobalt beads of the row.

11 Pass through the button once more. Weave around the beadwork edge, passing through the button a third time, then secure any remaining thread and trim.

12 Remove the stop bead from the start of the beadwork and weave around the edge of the net to exit between the ruby and cobalt blocks, 2 rows back from the edge.

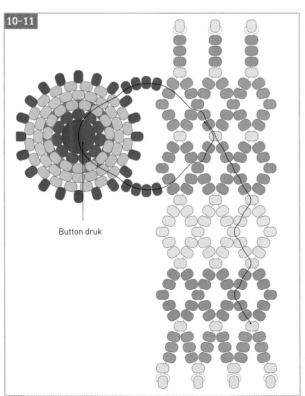

Button druk

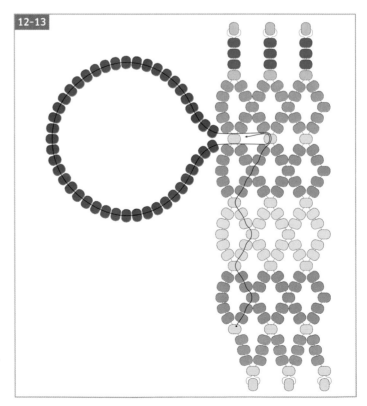

13 Pick up 40 to 45 ruby seed beads and pass through the topaz bead to form a loop. Test the fit of the loop on the button, adding or removing beads as necessary. Pass through the loop twice, then secure any remaining thread and trim.

14 Thread a needle on a new 2-yd (1.8-m) length of beading line. Attach a stop bead, leaving an 8-in. (20-cm) tail. Secure the thread at one end of the net, and exit from the top of the last fringe, facing away from the beadwork.

15 Pick up 4 topaz beads. Stitch back through the first topaz just added and the top fringe bead. Pull snug to form a picot.

16 Pick up 2 topaz beads and pass through the topaz at the top of the next fringe. Repeat 4 times.

17 Weave down through the current fringe and around the red nets, exit up through the previous fringe, and pass through the topaz beads just added. Add 5 more pairs of topaz beads between fringes.

18 Repeat step 17 along the entire edge. Exit from the top of the final fringe and pick up 4 topaz beads. Stitch back through the first bead just added, and weave back into the new row of topaz beads. Weave any remaining thread back through the edge, turning through the netting several times, as in step 17. Secure the last few inches of thread in netting and trim.

Bead selection: Czech glass seed beads work best for this design. Their smaller, more subtle shape allows the netting to fit closely together, creating the illusion of a solid piece, like the collar worn in the pharaoh's funerary mask.

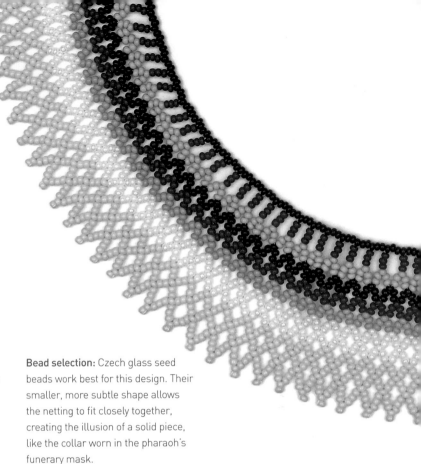

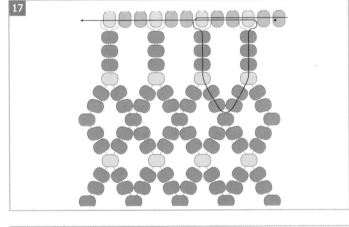

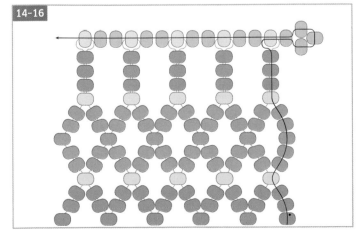

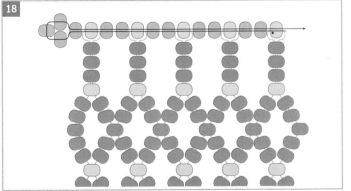

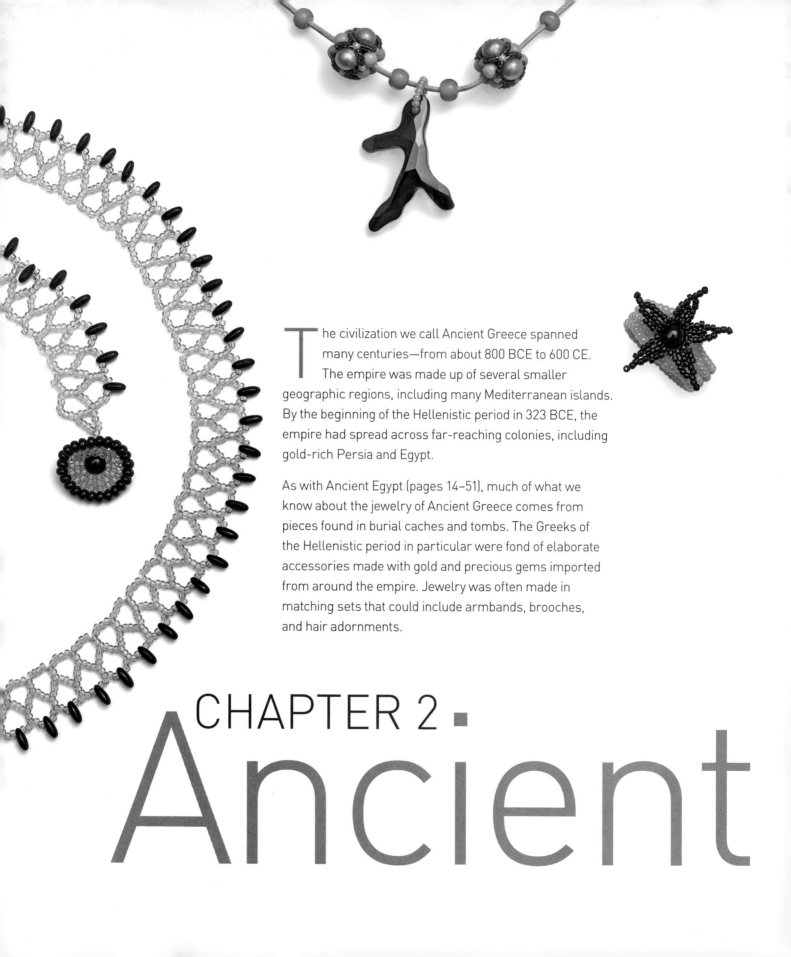

The civilization we call Ancient Greece spanned many centuries—from about 800 BCE to 600 CE. The empire was made up of several smaller geographic regions, including many Mediterranean islands. By the beginning of the Hellenistic period in 323 BCE, the empire had spread across far-reaching colonies, including gold-rich Persia and Egypt.

As with Ancient Egypt (pages 14–51), much of what we know about the jewelry of Ancient Greece comes from pieces found in burial caches and tombs. The Greeks of the Hellenistic period in particular were fond of elaborate accessories made with gold and precious gems imported from around the empire. Jewelry was often made in matching sets that could include armbands, brooches, and hair adornments.

CHAPTER 2 ·
Ancient

As the support for luxury items grew throughout the centuries, so too did the talent of jewelry artists. In addition to simple bezel settings and shapes, artisans began incorporating elaborate motifs into their bracelets, earrings, and necklaces. The development of gem-carving techniques led to the invention of the signet ring and the cameo, which still appear in jewelry today.

In this chapter, we'll use seed bead palettes and unique accents to capture the island vibe of the Mediterranean region. Ancient Greek jewelry styles are recreated with modern beadweaving techniques to make statement jewelry that exudes a royal elegance.

Greece

Perseus Pendant

Perseus (pictured here triumphantly holding the head of Medusa) was a character in Greek legend credited with the creation of coral, which continues to inspire jewelry designers to this day. This project combines tropical Mediterranean blue with a gorgeous coral pendant and beaded beads—one of the greatest assets in a beadweaver's repertoire. Endlessly varied and versatile, even the simplest combinations of beads and stitches can make for fabulous beadwork focal points that are unique to your projects.

SKILL LEVEL: BEGINNER
TECHNIQUE: STRINGING

TOOLS AND MATERIALS

- 32 in. (81 cm) 1.5 mm sea blue waxed cotton cord
- 75 in. (1.9 m) crystal braided beading line, 6 lb test (size D)
- Size 10 and 13 beading needles

Beads
- 1 x 40 mm mauve red crystal coral pendant (1)
- 8 x 6 mm sea blue freshwater pearls (2)
- 16 x 4 mm turquoise glass druks (3)
- 4 x 5 mm turquoise white-heart beads (4)
- 3 g pearl light cream 11/0 seed beads (5)
- 128 mauve-lined topaz 15/0 seed beads (6)

Dimensions: 28–30 in. (71–76 cm)

COLOR PALETTE

1	2	3
4	5	6

1 Using your pearls and druks, create 2 beaded beads (Techniques page 136) and set aside. Thread a needle on 15 in. (38 cm) of braided line, and attach a stop bead with a 6-in. (15-cm) tail. Pick up 6 size 11 seed beads, and slide them down to the end.

2 Needle through the coral pendant and carefully slide the seed beads through the hole.

Pick up 10 more seed beads. Stitch through the first 3 beads added in step 1, and pull snug to form a simple looped bail.

3 Carefully weave through the loop twice, moving a few beads at a time, tying a half-hitch knot between beads after the first pass (Techniques, page 131). Weave through a few beads and trim the thread.

4 Remove the stop bead and repeat step 3 to weave in the tail.

5 Gently stretch your cotton cord, then string 1 white-heart, 1 beaded bead, 1 white-heart, and the coral pendant. Repeat the pattern with the other beads.

6 Tie the cord with sliding knots (Techniques, page 131) and adjust to the length desired.

Stitch help: Size 15 seed beads should be large enough to take several thread passes. If you find that it is too difficult to stitch through a bead when weaving in the threads, switch to a size 13 needle.

Bead selection: Look for the roundest pearls and the most uniform seed beads to get perfectly proportioned beaded beads.

Variations: For a really fast design, replace the beaded beads with lampwork spacers or your favorite large-hole beads.

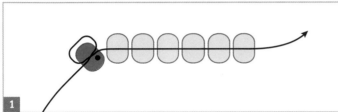

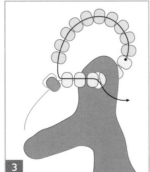

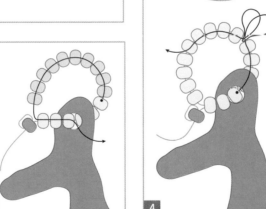

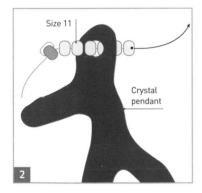

Size 11

Crystal pendant

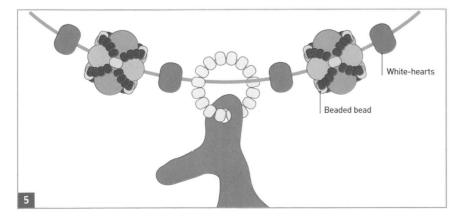

White-hearts

Beaded bead

Laurel Bracelet

The laurel wreath—made from branches of bay laurel—was a type of Ancient Greek trophy, given out for many achievements, such as poetic skill or athletic prowess in the Olympics. Later adopted by the Romans, it also became a symbol of military honor. This bracelet combines the unique structure of a double-layer St. Petersburg chain with the natural appeal of a leaf fringe. The result is a delicate-looking bracelet fit for Apollo.

TOOLS AND MATERIALS

- 6 yd (5.5 m) crystal braided beading line, 6 lb test (size D)
- Size 10 beading needle

Beads
- 3 g light topaz 11/0 seed beads (1)
- 3 g dark green 11/0 seed beads (2)
- 2 g dark green 8/0 seed beads (3)
- 1 x 6 mm topaz druk bead (1)

Dimensions: 1 x 7 in. (2.5 x 17 cm)

COLOR PALETTE

| 1 | 2 | 3 |

1 Thread a needle on 2 yd (1.8 m) of beading thread, and attach a stop bead, leaving an 8-in. (20-cm) tail. Pick up 6 topaz seed beads, and slide them down to the stop bead.

2 Keeping the beads tight against the stop, stitch up through the third and fourth beads added, and carefully pull the thread snug to form a little P shape.

3 Pick up 1 topaz seed bead. Stitch down through the fourth, third, and second bead added in step 1, and pull snug.

4 Pick up one size 8 bead and stitch up through the fifth and sixth beads added—the two beads at the outside of the P shape.

5 Pick up 2 topaz and 2 green size 11 beads and slide them down to the beadwork. Stitch up through the 2 topaz beads added, and pull snug to form a new P-shaped stitch, with the green beads on the outside.

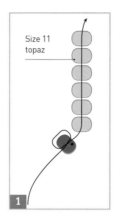

Size 11 topaz

1

2

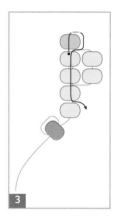

3

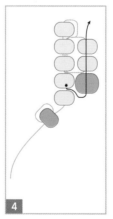

4

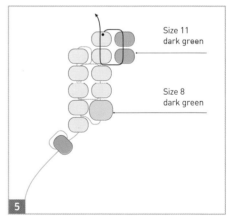

Size 11 dark green

Size 8 dark green

5

Variations: Although topaz and green give a very traditional look to this bracelet, leaf stitch looks fabulous in any color. Try making a bracelet for every season.

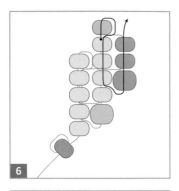

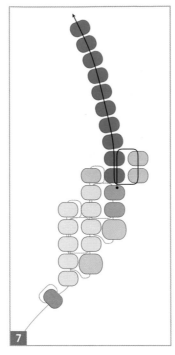

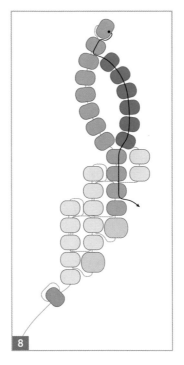

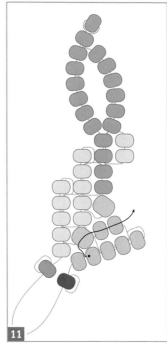

Play with patterns: For a leafier look, you can increase the size of your leaves, add more beads at the base for a stem, or even add a leaf to every row in the chain.

6 Pick up 1 topaz seed bead and stitch down through 3 beads as before. Pick up 1 size 8 bead and stitch up through the 2 green beads just added.

7 Pick up 2 green and 2 topaz beads and stitch up through the 2 green. Pick up 8 green seed beads and slide them down to the work.

8 Skipping the last bead added, stitch back through the seventh bead and pull snug. Pick up 6 green seed beads and stitch through 3 green beads in the base chain. Pull snug to form a leaf shape.

9 Pick up 1 size 8 seed bead and stitch up through the following 2 topaz seed beads in the chain. Repeat steps 5 through 9 until your chain is about 6½ in. (16.5 cm) long. Finish with a topaz row, and

pick up 4 topaz beads in the final stitch. Add the size 8 bead and stitch up through the next 2 topaz beads, then set the chain aside. Do not weave in the thread.

10 Attach a stop bead to a new length of thread, leaving an 8-in. (20-cm) tail. Repeat steps 1 to 3 to start a new St. Petersburg chain.

11 Instead of adding a new size 8 bead, carefully stitch up through the first size 8 bead of the first chain, and follow through the 2 topaz beads of the new chain. Pull the thread snug and check to make sure that the beadwork looks symmetrical.

12 Continue adding rows and leaves to the new chain with the same pattern, connecting each stitch to the corresponding size 8 bead in the first chain. Finish with 2 topaz rows as before.

13 Use your druk bead and size 11 seed beads to create a button clasp (Techniques, page 138).

14 Thread a needle on 1 tail from the beginning of the chain. Pass through the stop bead to remove it, and pick up 1 topaz seed bead and 1 size 8 bead.

15 Add 36 to 46 topaz seed beads and stitch through the size 8 bead added in step 14. Test the fit of the loop on your button, and add or remove beads as needed.

16 Pick up 1 topaz seed bead, and stitch through all of the topaz beads on the opposite side of the chain, being careful not to stitch through the stop bead.

17 Weave the thread back through the beadwork and around the clasp loop to secure. Weave any remaining thread

into the chain to secure it and trim. Remove the stop bead from the other tail and weave it through the clasp loop and into the beadwork. Trim.

18 Thread a needle on a tail at the opposite end of the bracelet. Pick up 4 topaz seed beads, needle through the druk from the back of the clasp button, and pick up 4 more topaz beads. Stitch through the final 2 topaz beads on the opposite chain.

19 Weave through the beadwork and the button clasp at least once more, then weave into the bracelet and trim the thread. Weave the final tail thread through the button at least once, and secure it in the beadwork before trimming.

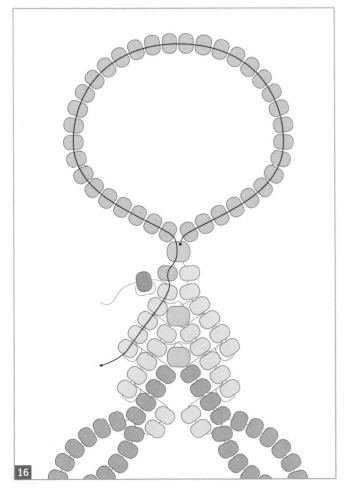

12

14

16

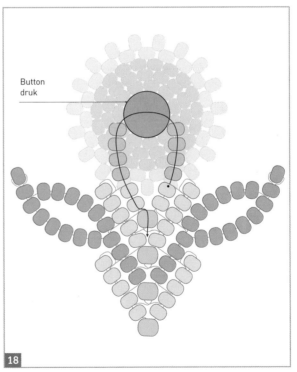

Button
druk

18

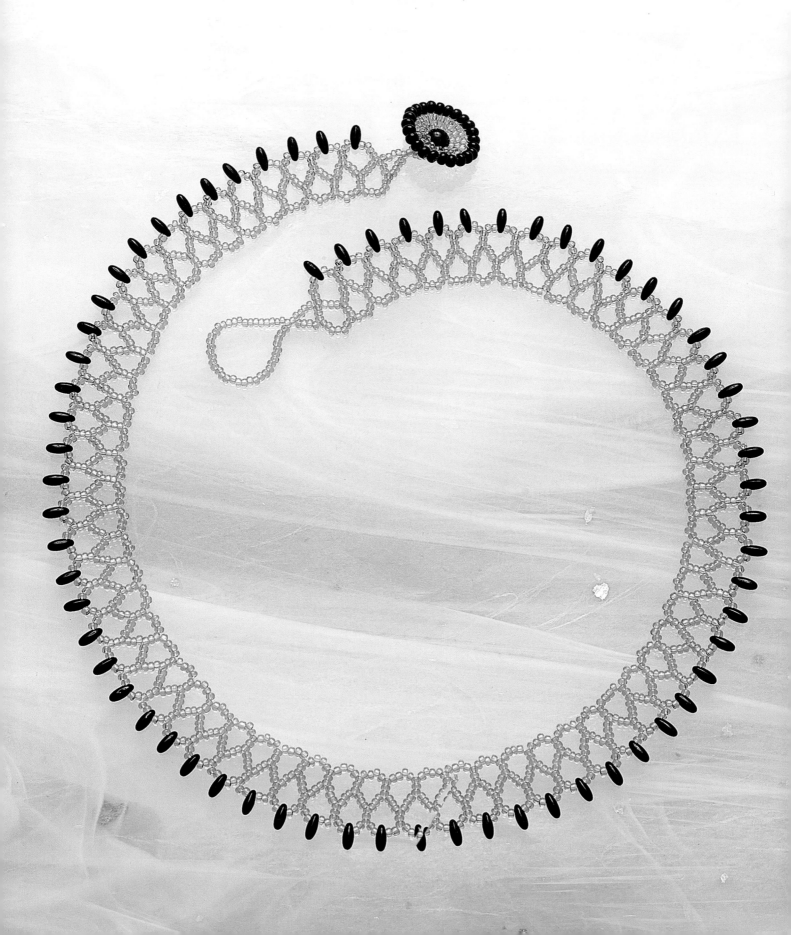

Helen of Troy Collar

Many necklaces dating back to Ancient Greece feature a beautiful fringed design reminiscent of Egyptian nefer-bead collars, such as the Hellenistic-era necklace seen right. This project features a simplified variation that can be stitched in a day, using delightful rice-shaped drop beads and chevron chain—a uniquely structured form of netting. The curved shape of this necklace is achieved by increasing the number of beads on one side, allowing room for the fringe accents.

SKILL LEVEL: **INTERMEDIATE**
TECHNIQUE: **CHEVRON CHAIN**

TOOLS AND MATERIALS

- 5 yd (4.5 m) crystal braided beading line, 6 lb test (size D)
- Size 10 beading needle

Beads
- 8 g transparent light topaz 11/0 seed beads (1)
- 68 x 2.5 mm black rice drop beads (2)
- 1 x 6 mm black druk bead (2)
- 3 g black 8/0 seed beads (2)

Dimensions: ¾ x 20 in. (2 x 50 cm)

COLOR PALETTE

1   2

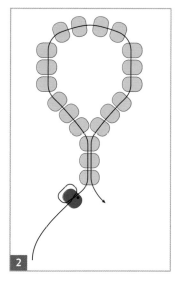

1 Create a clasp button with a square stitch trim (Techniques, pages 138). Set aside. Attach a stop bead to 2 yd (1.8 m) of beading line, leaving a 10-in. (25-cm) tail. Pick up 19 seed beads, and slide them down to the end.

2 Stitch down through the first 3 seed beads added, and pull snug. Your beadwork should take on a half-hourglass shape.

3 Pick up 2 seed beads, 1 rice drop, and 8 seed beads. Skipping the closest 6 beads in the beadwork, stitch up through 3 seed beads and pull snug.

4 Pick up 10 seed beads. Skipping the 3 beads you just stitched through and the last 3 beads added in the previous step, stitch down through 3 seed beads, and pull snug.

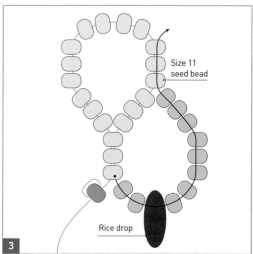

Size 11 seed bead

Rice drop

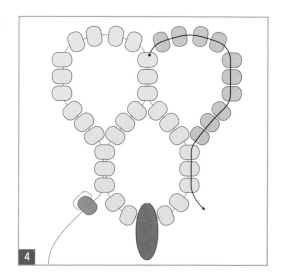

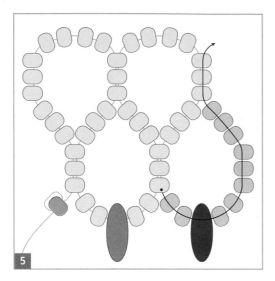

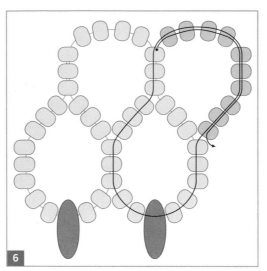

5 Pick up 2 seed beads, 1 rice drop, and 8 seed beads. Skip over the closest 6 seed beads in the beadwork, and stitch up through the following 3 seed beads.

6 Repeat steps 4 and 5 until all of the rice drops have been added, starting new threads as necessary. Finish the chain with a 10 seed bead stitch and weave around to exit from the last bead added.

7 Pick up 40 to 50 seed beads. Stitch back through the fifth and sixth bead just added and pull snug to form the clasp loop. Test the fit of the loop on the button clasp, adding or removing beads as necessary.

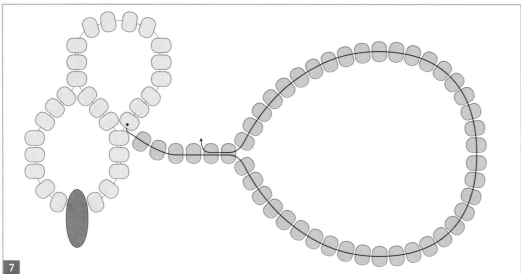

8 Pick up 4 seed beads, and stitch through the last 3 beads added in the chevron chain. Weave through the loop at least once more, following the natural thread path of the beadwork. Secure the thread in the chevron chain and trim.

9 Remove the stop bead from the first tail thread. Weave around the first stitch to exit from the same start position as in step 6.

> **Bead selection:** If you choose another type of drop bead for an accent, try to use beads that are no larger than size 8 seed beads, to maintain the right curve in the beadwork.

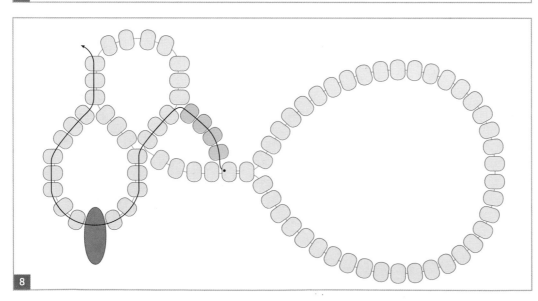

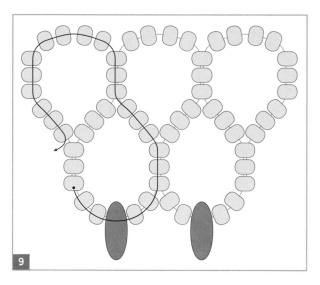

9

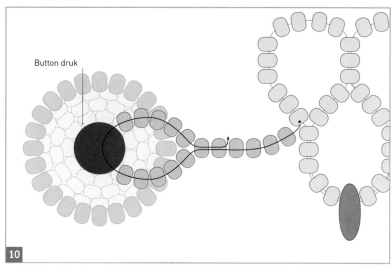

Button druk

10

10 Pick up 11 seed beads, pass through the button druk, and pick up 5 seed beads. Stitch back through the sixth and seventh seed bead behind the button and pull snug.

11 Pick up 4 beads, and stitch through the center 3 beads of the first chevron stitch.

12 Weave through the button clasp at least once more to add strength, then secure the thread in the chevron chain and trim. Weave in any remaining tail threads.

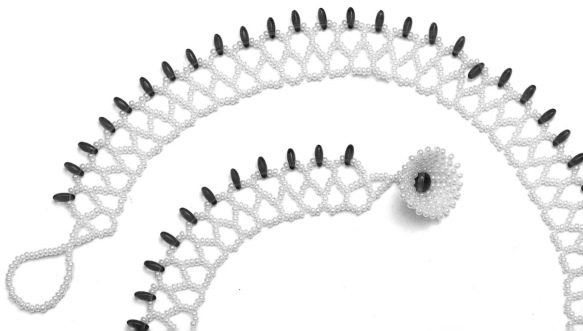

11

Securing your beadwork: This variation of the chevron chain is light and airy. When weaving in your threads, it is a good idea to tie one or two half-hitch knots within 3-bead sections at the center of the beadwork.

Crescent Earrings

Crescent-shaped earrings are a common sight among the Greek collections of the world's museums, with beautiful combinations of gold and precious gems. Many pieces also feature another classic element—three or more evenly spaced dangles or drops. The crescent shape is elegant and feminine, making it ideal for dangling statement earrings. This project combines shimmering pearls with seed beads for a beachy empress look.

TOOLS AND MATERIALS

- 2 x 20-gauge 6 mm silver filled jump rings
- 2 x 20-gauge silver filled earwires
- 4 yd (3.6 m) crystal braided beading line, 6 lb test (size D)
- Size 10 beading needle

Beads

- 2 x 8 mm sea blue freshwater potato pearls (1)
- 6 x 5 mm gold freshwater potato pearls (2)
- 2 x 6 mm transparent aqua glass druks (3)
- 2 g transparent aqua 11/0 seed beads (3)
- 2 g transparent dark topaz 11/0 seed beads (4)

Dimensions: 1¼ x 3¼ in. (3 x 8 cm)

COLOR PALETTE

1	2
3	4

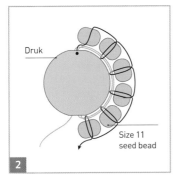

1 On 2 yd (1.8 m) of beading line, string one druk and slide it to the end, leaving a 6-in. (15-cm) tail. Pass up through the druk twice and pull snug to form a double bridge of thread on one side. Using circular brick stitch (Techniques, page 137) create a base row across one half of the bead in transparent blue seed beads.

2 Stitch up through the final bead added in the row. Pick up 2 blue seed beads, and stitch under the nearest bridge. Stitch up through the second bead added. Continue adding beads with brick stitch until you reach the end of the row. To make sure that the rows do not decrease too dramatically and alter the crescent shape, add a second bead to the last bridge thread in each new row.

3 Add a third row of brick stitch in blue, and 3 rows in topaz. Add a final row in blue.

4 To make the dangles symmetrical, find the center point of the outside row. Count the number of beads in the outer blue row. If it is an even number, subtract 6 and divide the result by 2. This will determine how many short fringes to add in the next step. If the number is odd, subtract 5, then divide by 2.

5 Pick up 2 blue seed beads. Skipping the second bead, stitch through the first bead just picked up and through the same bead in the base row that your thread is exiting. Pull snug to form a short fringe.

Securing your beadwork: To prevent the threads of the loop from slipping through the opening of the jump ring, coat the seed bead loop with a dab of clear nail polish, or thread on a soldered jump ring in step 13, before closing the loop. To finish the earring, add additional jump rings for the length and drape you want.

Druk

Size 11 seed bead

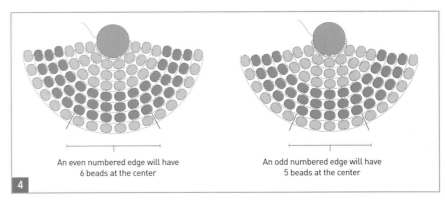

An even numbered edge will have 6 beads at the center

An odd numbered edge will have 5 beads at the center

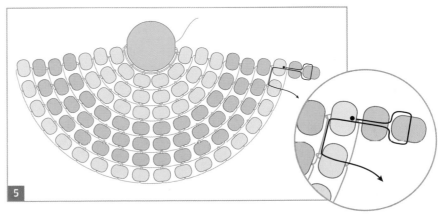

CRESCENT EARRINGS

6 Stitch up through the next bead in the base row. Pick up 2 beads, and stitch back through the first bead and the base row. Continue adding fringes to one third of the crescent.

7 Stitch up through the next bead in the base row. Pick up 9 blue beads, 1 gold pearl, and 2 blue beads. Skipping the last bead added, stitch back through all of the beads again, and into the base row. Carefully pull the thread snug to form the first dangle.

8 Stitch up through the base row and add a short fringe with 2 blue beads.

9 Exit from the next bead in the base row. Add 12 blue seed beads, 1 gold pearl, and 2 blue seed beads.

10 If your base row has an even number, skip the last bead added, and stitch through the next seed bead, pearl, and 11 blue seed beads. Pick up 1 seed bead, and stitch into the next available bead in the base row (a). If the base row has an odd number, skip the last bead added in the fringe, and pass through all of the remaining beads and into the base (b). Pull snug to form the center fringe.

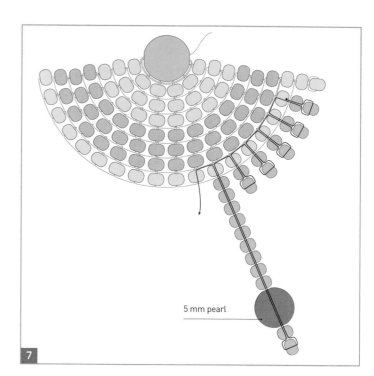

5 mm pearl

7

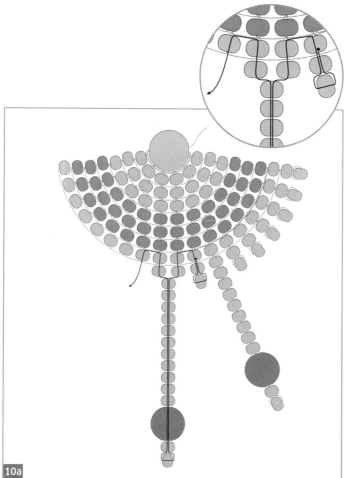

10a

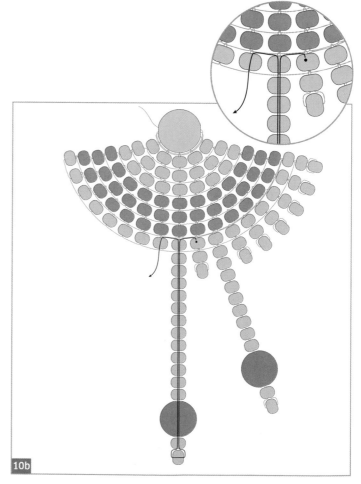

10b

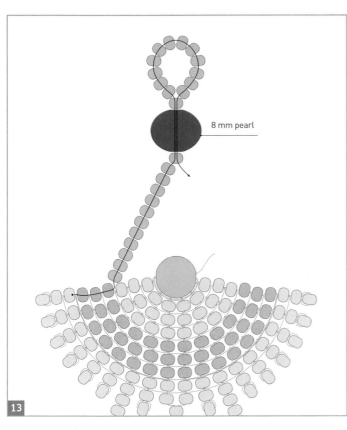

11 Add 1 short fringe with 2 beads and 1 pearl fringe with 9 beads as in step 7.

12 Add short fringes to the remaining beads in the base row. After adding the last fringe, stitch through the base row and the following 3 topaz beads to exit the top edge.

13 Pick up 12 blue seed beads, 1 blue pearl, and 13 blue seed beads. Skipping the last 12 beads just added, stitch through 1 seed bead, the pearl and the following seed bead. Pull snug to form a loop.

14 Pick up 11 seed beads and weave into the 3 topaz beads on the opposite edge and through the fringe beads.

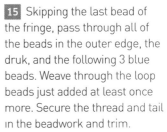

Variations: If you'd like to make the pearl fringes extra long for shoulder-duster earrings, switch to unwaxed nylon beading thread in step 5 for more supple fringing. You may wish to wax the thread before stitching in the top loop, to make it more durable.

15 Skipping the last bead of the fringe, pass through all of the beads in the outer edge, the druk, and the following 3 blue beads. Weave through the loop beads just added at least once more. Secure the thread and tail in the beadwork and trim.

16 Open a jump ring. Thread on the topmost loop of the dangle and 1 earwire. Close the jump ring securely. Repeat to make a second earring.

8 mm pearl

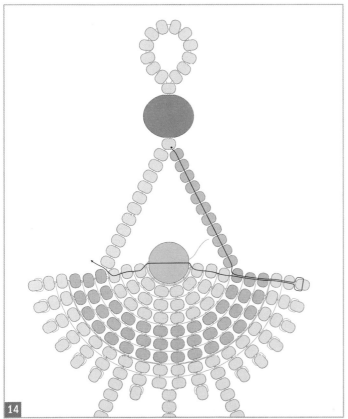

Earwire

Jump ring

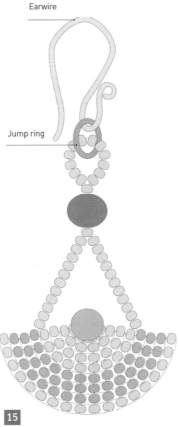

Cassiopeia Coil Bracelet

The coiled armband is one of the most recognized styles of classical jewelry. This project mimics the design in a simpler form, allowing for fun color combinations with a two-tone beaded rope and coil-like embellishments. Using two slightly different bead sizes with tubular herringbone weave creates a gentle curve that is perfect for bangles and bracelets. By combining Czech and Japanese seed beads, you can create a rope with a single color, or use a contrast for an even bolder look.

SKILL LEVEL: INTERMEDIATE
TECHNIQUE: TUBULAR HERRINGBONE WEAVE

TOOLS AND MATERIALS

- 19 yd (17.3 m) white nylon beading thread, size D
- Beading wax
- Size 10 beading needle

Beads
- 8 g light topaz 11/0 Japanese seed beads (1)
- 6 g medium topaz 11/0 Czech seed beads (2)
- 2 g brown iris 11/0 Czech seed beads (3)
- 2 x 6 mm brown iris glass druks (4)
- 1 x 18 mm hematite Czech glass button (5)

Dimensions: ½ x 7½ in. (1 x 19 cm)

COLOR PALETTE

1	2	3
4	5	

1 Thread a needle onto 50 in. (1.2 m) of waxed beading thread. Leaving a 14-in. (35-cm) tail, create an 8-stack-wide 2-bead ladder in topaz with the following pattern: 1 Czech bead, 5 Japanese beads, and 2 Czech beads (a), (Techniques, page 132). Use ladder stitch to weave the first and last stacks together securely (b), then stitch up through the first stack of Czech beads added.

2 Add 8 beads around the top of the ladder using herringbone weave, making sure to match the beads to the ones in the ladder below (a). Step up by stitching up through the top 2 beads of the first stack (b).

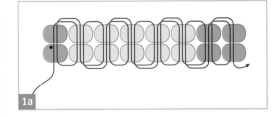

1a

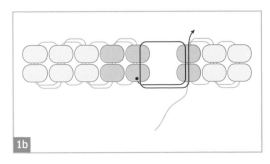

1b

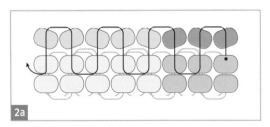

2a

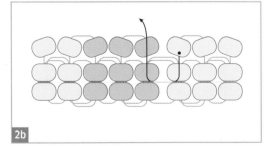

2b

3 Continue adding rounds of tubular herringbone (Techniques, page 133), following the bead pattern of 5 Japanese beads and 3 Czech beads. Add new thread as needed, until the rope is 1½ in. (4 cm) short of the desired length of your bracelet.

4 Use the herringbone dummy stitch (Techniques, page 133) to secure the final 2 rounds, and seal the top of the tube (a). Stitch down through the nearest column, and exit 4 beads down (b).

5 Pass the needle between the beads and into the center of the tube (a). Exit from the top and pick up one druk. Add 35–40 seed beads (b).

6 Stitch back through the first seed bead added and the druk, and pass the needle through the tube on the opposite side. Pull snug to form the clasp loop. Test the fit of the loop on the button, adding or removing beads as necessary.

7 Stitch down through the nearest 3 seed beads in the tube, then up through the following 3 seed beads. Pass the needle through the tube and carefully stitch back up through the druk bead. Weave through the loop and back into the tube. Repeat once more.

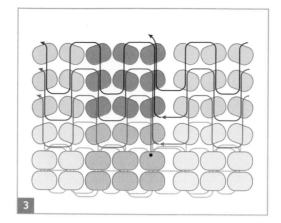

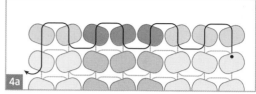

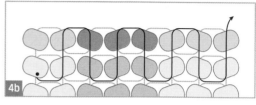

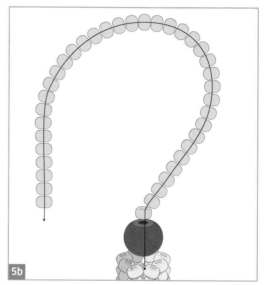

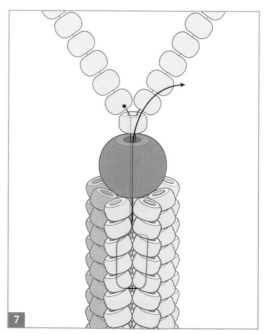

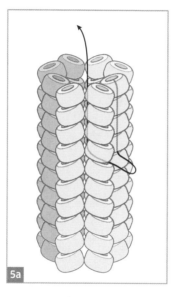

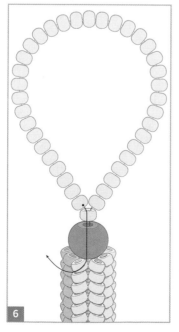

8 Exit from the top of the herringbone tube. Pick up 3 seed beads, matching them to the beads in the columns below. Stitch down into the following column. Repeat around the tube to add 4 more 3-bead picots.

9 Weave up to exit from the closest picot, and stitch through all 3 beads. Pick up 1 seed bead, and pass through the next picot. Repeat to add 3 more beads. Weave around the entire ring of picots again, passing through the picots and new beads added, then secure the thread in the herringbone tube and trim.

10 Thread the needle on the tail thread and repeat steps 5 through 9 to add the button with a base of 4 beads plus 2, as shown. Add the picot trim and weave in any remaining thread.

11 Add a stop bead to 20 in. (50 cm) of waxed thread, leaving a 4-in. (10-cm) tail. Pick up 15 seed beads in any color. Wrap the beads around the tube. Add or remove beads to make a loop that just fits around the tube, with a bit of room to spare. Your loop should be snug but not tight. When in doubt, add more beads.

12 Pass through the first few beads, and pull snug to form the loop. Weave around the loop 3 times, adding a knot between beads in the second pass. Trim the thread. Repeat to add 4 more loops in alternating colors.

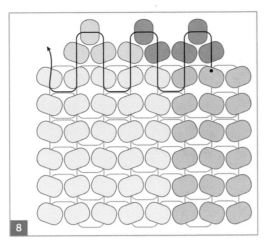

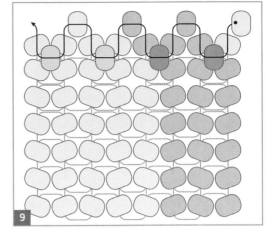

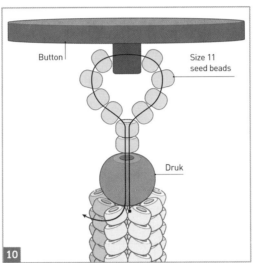

Button

Size 11 seed beads

Druk

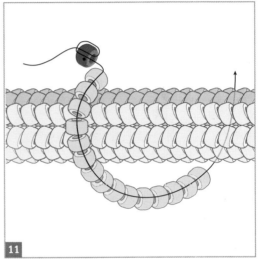

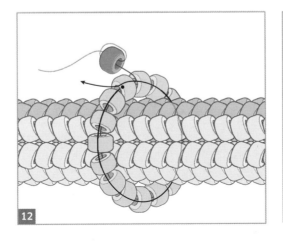

Stitch help: When adding your loop embellishment, be sure that your loops are fairly snug, but not too tight. Once you've woven in the thread, loops that are too small will have a lot of exposed thread showing. The picot trim at the ends of the tube are big enough to stop all but the most generous loops, so don't worry about adding an extra seed bead or two.

Demeter Bib Necklace

The Greek goddess Demeter—whose statue is seen here in Sintra, Portugal—was the embodiment of vegetation, agriculture, and the forces of life and death. She was sometimes referred to as the Earth Mother. Light and airy right-angle weave is a perfect stitch for statement jewelry dedicated to a garden goddess. This design features short RAW chain straps for a choker-like fit that you could wear with a toga.

SKILL LEVEL: INTERMEDIATE
TECHNIQUE: OPENWORK
RIGHT-ANGLE WEAVE (RAW)

TOOLS AND MATERIALS

- 9 yd (8.2 m) smoke braided beading line, 6 lb test (size D)
- Size 10 beading needle

Beads

- 10 g transparent dark green 11/0 seed beads (1)
- 2 g transparent lime green 11/0 seed beads (2)
- 10 Picasso yellow fringe drops (3)
- 3 x 2.5 mm Picasso green rice drops (4)

Dimensions: 3 x 15 in. (7.5 x 38 cm)

COLOR PALETTE

1	2
3	4

1 On 2 yd (1.8 m) of beading line, string a pattern of 3 dark green and 1 lime green bead 3 times. Add 3 dark green beads and 1 yellow drop (a). Pass through all of the beads again to form a circle, leaving an 8-in. (20-cm) tail. Weave through the next 4 beads to exit a lime green bead (b).

2 Pick up 3 dark green and 1 lime green bead 3 times and add 3 dark green beads. Stitch through the lime green bead that the thread is exiting and the following 8 beads in the link just added, exiting from a lime green bead.

3 Repeat step 2 to make a total of 10 links. For the final link, pick up 3 dark green and 1 drop, 3 dark green and 1 lime green twice, and 3 more dark green. Pass through the lime green bead that the thread is

exiting, pass through the following 3 dark green beads of the previous link, and exit through the next lime green bead.

4 Pick up 3 dark green and 1 lime green bead 3 times and 3 more dark green beads. Stitch through the base lime green bead and then through the first 4 beads just added.

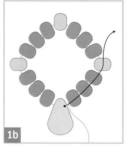

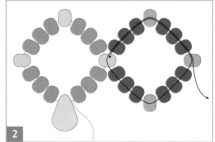

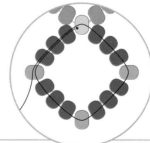

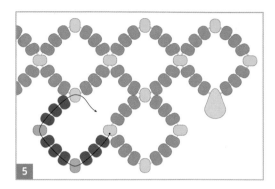

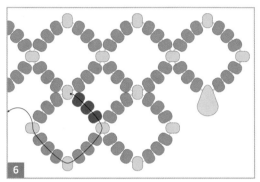

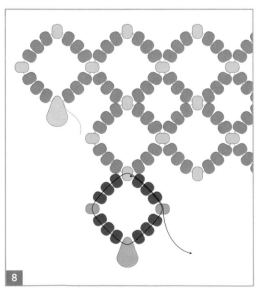

5 Pick up 3 dark green and 1 lime green twice, plus 3 dark green beads. Stitch through the lowest lime green bead of the link in the previous row and pull snug to form part of a new link.

6 Pick up 3 dark green and stitch through the next lime green bead, in the first link added for this row. Pass through the following 8 beads to exit from a lime green bead.

7 Pick up 3 dark green beads and stitch through the lowest lime green bead of the link above. To close the new link, add 3 dark green and 1 lime green twice, plus 3 dark green, and stitch through the leftmost lime green of the previous link. Pass through the following 8 beads.

8 Repeat steps 5 through 7 to make a total of 9 links in this row. Exit from the lowest lime green of the link just added. Pick up 3 dark green, 1 lime green, 3 dark green, 1 drop, 3 dark green, 1 lime green, and 3 dark green. Weave through the new link to exit the rightmost lime green bead.

9 Add 7 links with RAW and a final link with 1 drop at the lowest point. Weave around to exit from the lowest lime green of the previous link.

10 Add 7 dark green and lime green links to the new row, then exit from the lowest lime green of the final link. Add 1 link with a rice bead at the lowest point, 5 plain links, and 1 rice link. Exit from the bottom of the previous link.

11 Add 5 plain links to the new row. For the following row, add 1 drop link, 3 plain, and 1 drop link.

12 Exit from the lowest point of the previous link. Add 3 plain links to the next row. For the following row, add 1 drop, 1 plain, and 1 drop link.

13 Exit from the center link and add 1 link with a rice bead at the bottom. Weave around the final link twice and secure all remaining thread and tails in the beadwork, keeping to the edges.

14 Create a toggle clasp 12 beads long in emerald, with lime trim (Techniques, page 134), and set aside.

15 Secure a new 2-yd (1.8-m) thread in the beadwork with a 6-in. (15-cm) tail, and exit from the topmost lime green of the second link in the top row, facing outward.

16 Pick up 3 dark green, 1 drop, 3 dark green and 1 lime green twice, plus 3 dark green. Pass through the base lime green bead and the first 8 beads of the new link.

17 Repeat step 16 to add a single chain of 15 links using only dark green and lime green beads. Exit from the topmost lime green bead of the last link, and pick up 34 dark green seed beads. Stitch through the base lime green bead, and pass through the loop twice more. Test the fit of the loop on the toggle, adding or removing beads as necessary. Weave the remaining thread into the chain.

18 Repeat step 15 on the opposite side of the beadwork. Add 1 drop link and 15 plain links, and exit from the topmost lime green bead of the final link.

19 Pick up 3 dark green, 1 lime green, and 3 dark green. Pass through 2 beads at the center of the toggle. Add 3 dark green, 1 lime green, and 3 dark green. Pass through the base lime green in the final link. Weave through the toggle loop twice, and pass through the beadwork in the toggle once. Weave back into the chain, and secure any remaining thread.

9

Variations: If you prefer a longer necklace, simply increase the number of links in both chain straps. For extra texture, include drops all the way along the chains.

Stitch help: If you're not familiar with right-angle weave, the steps can seem a bit confusing until you find your own beading rhythm. If you get lost, remember that each new link is also a complete circle of 16 beads—but with any adjacent lime green beads being shared from previous rows.

Fringe drop

Size 11 dark green

Size 11 lime

Rice drop

10

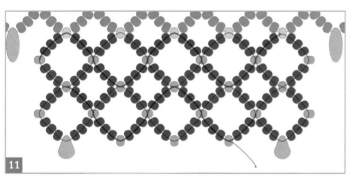

11

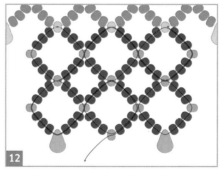

12

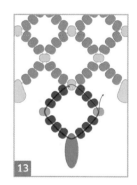

13

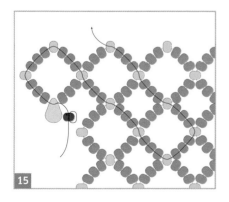

15

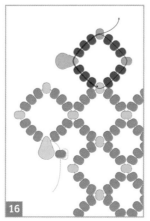

16

17

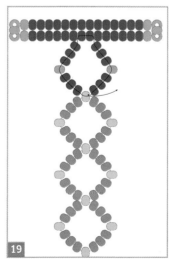

19

Atlantis Fringe Lariat

Though the sunken city of Atlantis may be the stuff of legends, the real-life Greek city of Heracleion (part of which is shown to the left) is a wonder to behold. Like the vessel shown left, the green patinas resulting from hundreds of years under the sea make the city's ancient statues look right at home in the tropical blue waters. This light but sturdy chevron chain lariat uses a blue-green ombre effect inspired by tropical treasures. The flexibility of the chain makes this necklace wearable in any number of styles—wrap it or knot it to channel your inner sea goddess.

SKILL LEVEL: INTERMEDIATE
TECHNIQUES: CHEVRON CHAIN, FRINGE

TOOLS AND MATERIALS

- 14 yd (12.8 m) crystal braided beading line, 6 lb test (size D)
- 6 yd (5.5 m) white nylon beading thread, size D
- Size 10 beading needle

Beads
- 6 x 7 mm chartreuse green glass rondelles (7)
- 6 x 6 mm turquoise blue glass white-hearts (2)
- 2 x 18 mm 3-dot glass ovals in aqua blue (1) and lime green (9)

Seed beads: 11/0
- 6 g transparent aqua blue (1)
- 6 g transparent mint green (8)
- 4 g transparent lime green (9)
- 4 g transparent sea blue (2)
- 3 g transparent cobalt blue (3)
- 3 g transparent Montana sapphire blue (4)
- 3 g transparent dark green (5)
- 3 g transparent emerald green (6)

Seed beads: 8/0
- 6 transparent emerald (6)
- 6 transparent cobalt (3)

Dimensions: ½ x 27 in. (1 x 69 cm)

COLOR PALETTE

1	2	3	4	
5	6	7	8	9

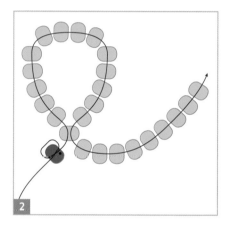

2

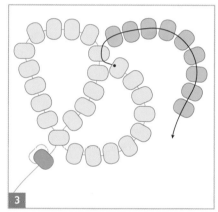

3

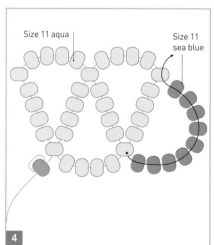

Size 11 aqua

Size 11 sea blue

4

1 Attach a stop bead to 2 yd (1.8 m) of beading line, leaving an 8-in. (20-cm) tail. Pick up 15 aqua blue seed beads.

2 Stitch back through the first bead added and pull snug to form a teardrop-shaped loop. Pick up 9 aqua seed beads.

3 Skipping the last 4 beads added, stitch up through the fifth bead (the eleventh bead added in step 1). Pick up 9 aqua beads, and stitch down through the fifth bead just added.

4 Pick up 9 sea blue seed beads, and stitch through the fifth aqua bead added in the previous step. Repeat to add 3 more stitches in sea blue.

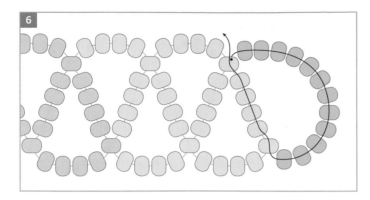

5 Add 4 stitches of each color in the following order: cobalt, sapphire, dark green, emerald, lime, mint, aqua, and sea blue. Repeat the pattern until the chain reaches about 50 in. (1.2 m) in length, adding new thread as needed.

6 Continue the color pattern, ending with 3 stitches of mint green. Add 12 mint green seed beads, passing through the fifth bead added in the previous stitch. Weave around the final stitches and pass through the last mint loop 3 times. Weave in any remaining thread.

7 Remove the stop bead from the beginning of the chain. Add 12 aqua seed beads and weave through the final loop 3 times. Secure the thread and all tails in the beadwork.

8 Attach a stop bead to 1 yd (0.9 m) of stretched unwaxed beading thread, leaving an 8-in. (20-cm) tail. Pick up 1 green size 8 bead, 1 green oval, 1 green size 8, and 75 sea blue seed beads. Stitch back up through the size 8 beads and oval to form a fringe loop.

9 Pick up 12 aqua seed beads and pass the thread through the final aqua loop of the chevron chain. Pass down through the size 8 beads and oval, and pull snug, making sure that the tassel and chevron loops have not crossed.

10 Pick up 75 aqua seed beads. Pass back through the size 8 beads and oval and the seed bead loop. Weave any remaining thread through the fringe, securing it with a half-hitch knot between beads, and trim.

11 Repeat steps 8 to 10 to add 2 more tassels, replacing the glass oval with 3 lime rondelles. Place the new tassels to either side of the first one, making sure not to cross or tangle the bead loops.

12 On the opposite end of the chevron chain, add 1 tassel using a blue oval and cobalt size 8 beads, with mint and lime green strands. Add 2 more tassels using 3 white-hearts in place of the oval.

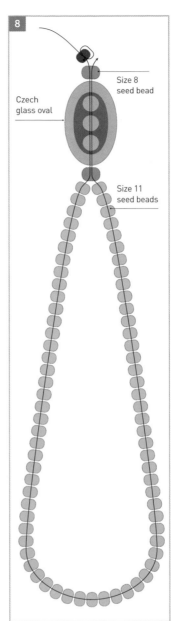

Size 8 seed bead

Czech glass oval

Size 11 seed beads

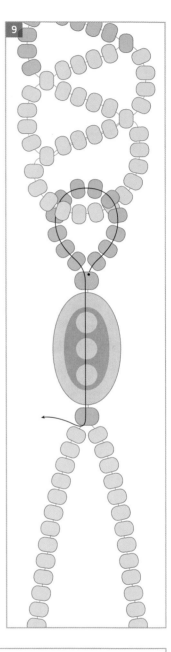

Securing your beadwork: When adding new thread, leave your tails long (10–12 in./25–30 cm) so that there will be plenty of extra thread to reinforce the chain. Weave old threads toward the start of the chain and new tails toward the opposite end.

Variations: To give your tassels a more organic look, vary the lengths or add additional fringes. You can also use straight fringe in place of the loops—see the Diana Earrings (page 98) for ideas.

Cyprus Sea Star Ring

Sea life was an important part of the culture and everyday life for the people of the ancient Mediterranean. From legends of sea monsters to gorgeous nautical art, the love and fear of the sea is apparent in many Greek works. This project is inspired by the bright red starfish and tropical blue waters of the Mediterranean. Mixing and altering beadwork stitches can result in amazing beaded treasures—this simple ring is easy to stitch once you know the steps and makes a wonderful accessory for sea lovers.

SKILL LEVEL: INTERMEDIATE
TECHNIQUES: MODIFIED CIRCULAR BRICK STITCH, MODIFIED HERRINGBONE WEAVE

TOOLS AND MATERIALS

- 2½ yd (2 m) smoke braided beading line, 6 lb test (size D)
- Size 11 and 13 beading needles

Beads
- 1 x 6 mm red glass druk (1)
- 2 g opaque red 15/0 seed beads (1)
- 2 g turquoise 11/0 seed beads (2)

Dimensions: ⅓ x 1 in. (8 x 25 mm)

COLOR PALETTE

1	2	

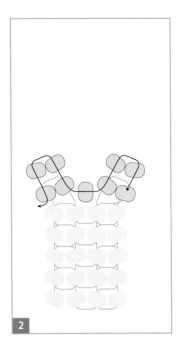

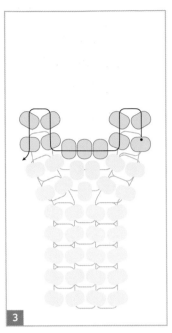

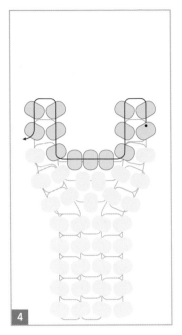

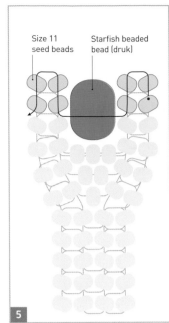

Size 11
seed beads

Starfish beaded
bead (druk)

1 Using the druk and size 15 beads, create a starfish bead (Techniques, page 139) and set aside. Thread a needle with 60 in. (1.5 m) of beading line, leaving a 6-in. (15-cm) tail. Create a 2-bead ladder with size 11 seed beads that is 4 columns wide, then add 16 rows of herringbone weave (Techniques, page 132).

2 Step up as usual for the next row and add 2 new beads with herringbone weave. Pick up 1 seed bead, then stitch up through the topmost bead of the next column to begin the next stitch for this row. Add 2 seed beads with herringbone weave, and step up.

3 Add 2 more rows of herringbone weave, adding 2 seed beads between the columns on the next row and 3 seed beads on the following row. Step up as usual.

4 Add 2 seed beads with herringbone, then pass through the 3 beads added to the increase in the last row. Stitch up through the top bead of the next column and add 2 beads with herringbone. Step up.

5 Add 2 beads, then pass the needle through the druk from the back of the starfish bead. Pull the thread snug, and push the starfish gently into the increase. Stitch up through the next column, and add 2 beads with herringbone stitch. Be sure to keep the thread snug as you step up for the next row.

Variations: This project looks great in aquatic hues, but don't stop there—try out your favorite color combinations. Use either black or crystal beading line for the starfish and ring, depending on your chosen colors.

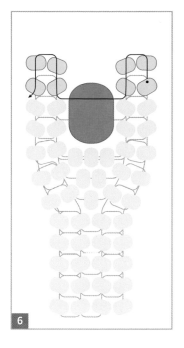

6

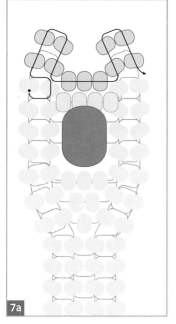

7a

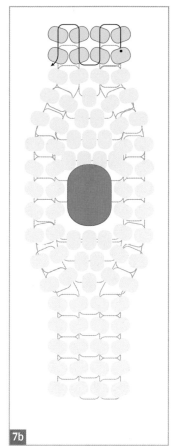

7b

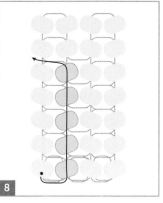

8

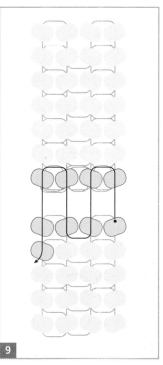

9

6 Add 2 beads with herringbone, and pass through the starfish bead again and up into the next column. Add another 2 beads, and step up.

7 In the next row, add 4 seed beads to the increase. Continue adding rows of herringbone, reducing the number of beads by one each time (a). After adding a row with a single bead in the increase, continue weaving with ordinary herringbone (b).

8 Test the fit of your ring against a sizing mandrel or your finger. When you have the desired length, thread a needle on the tail thread and stitch up through 4 or 5 beads to move the thread away from the edge.

9 Bring the ends of the beadwork together. Using the first needle, zip up the edges by weaving up and down through the first and last rows, one bead at a time. Pull snug after every stitch to create a smooth join.

10 Weave the thread across the join twice, following the natural herringbone thread path. Weave the remaining thread through the ring, passing several times through the starfish druk and the outermost columns of the beadwork. Repeat with the tail thread and trim.

Ring sizing: Weaving in the threads tightens up the beadwork and shrinks the ring. To resize it, gently stretch the finished ring over a mandrel or dowel before wearing. (See page 140 for standard ring sizes.)

SKILL LEVEL: ADVANCED
TECHNIQUES: NETTING, BEADED BEADS

TOOLS AND MATERIALS

- 23 yd (21 m) smoke braided beading line, 6 lb test (size D)
- 2 yd (1.8 m) crystal braided beading line, 6 lb test (size D)
- Size 10 beading needle

Beads
- 6 x 6 mm sea blue freshwater pearls (1)
- 8 x 6 mm turquoise blue freshwater pearls (2)
- 4 x 6 mm transparent lemon lime druks (3)
- 4 x 6 mm brown iris druks (4)
- 4 x 6 mm purple iris druks (5)
- 40 g jet black 11/0 seed beads (6)
- 20 g blue iris 11/0 seed beads (7)
- 8 g transparent amethyst 8/0 seed beads (5)
- 3 g black diamond 15/0 seed beads (4)
- 3 g transparent lemon lime 15/0 seed beads (3)
- 3 g purple-lined15/0 seed beads (5)

Dimensions: ½ x 7½ in.
(1 x 19 cm)

COLOR PALETTE

1	2	3
4	5	6	7

Nereid's Scarf Lariat

The Greek sea god Poseidon had a retinue of fifty water nymphs called the Nereids, each representing a different aspect of the sea. These beautiful sea creatures, depicted in the statue seen left, were thought to bring protection and aid to seafarers. This luxurious beaded scarf brings to mind a fisherman's net, glittering with jewels from the sea and capturing the allure of the mysterious ocean.

Project planning: You'll need to set aside at least an hour of beading time to start this project. Be sure to stitch the first 3 rows in one sitting to establish the netting and prevent tangling. A large workspace is recommended.

1 Use matching druks and size 15 seed beads to make 12 beaded starfish (Techniques, page 139) and set aside. Use crystal beading line for the lime starfish. In a small container, mix together the jet black and blue iris size 11 seed beads.

2 Cut 4 yd (3.6 m) of black beading line and add a stop bead with a 12-in. (30-cm) tail. Pick up a pattern of 1 size 8 and 12 size 11 seed beads 61 times to create the first row.

3 Add 1 size 8 bead and 14 of the seed beads. Skipping the last bead added, stitch back through the next bead and pull snug. Pick up 12 seed beads, 1 size 8, and 12 seed beads. Skipping the last size 8 added in row 1, pass through the following size 8 bead.

4 Pick up 12 seed beads, a starfish, and 12 seed beads. Skip 1 size 8 and stitch through the following size 8 of the first row. Add another plain net with 12 seed beads, 1 size 8, and 12 seed beads.

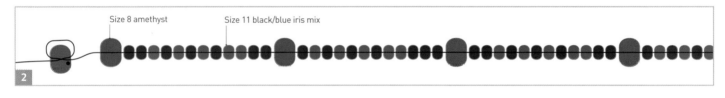

Size 8 amethyst · Size 11 black/blue iris mix

2

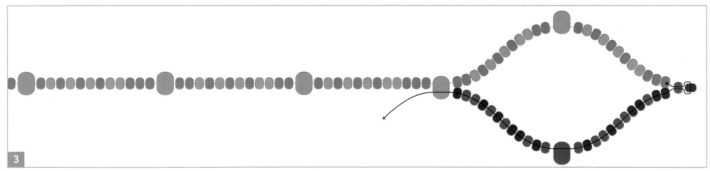

3

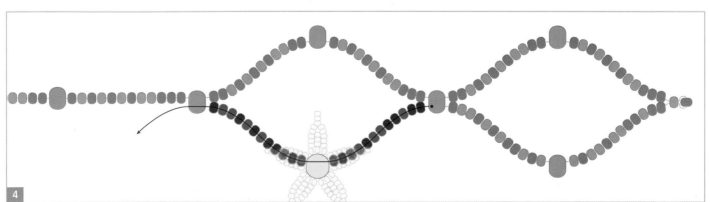

4

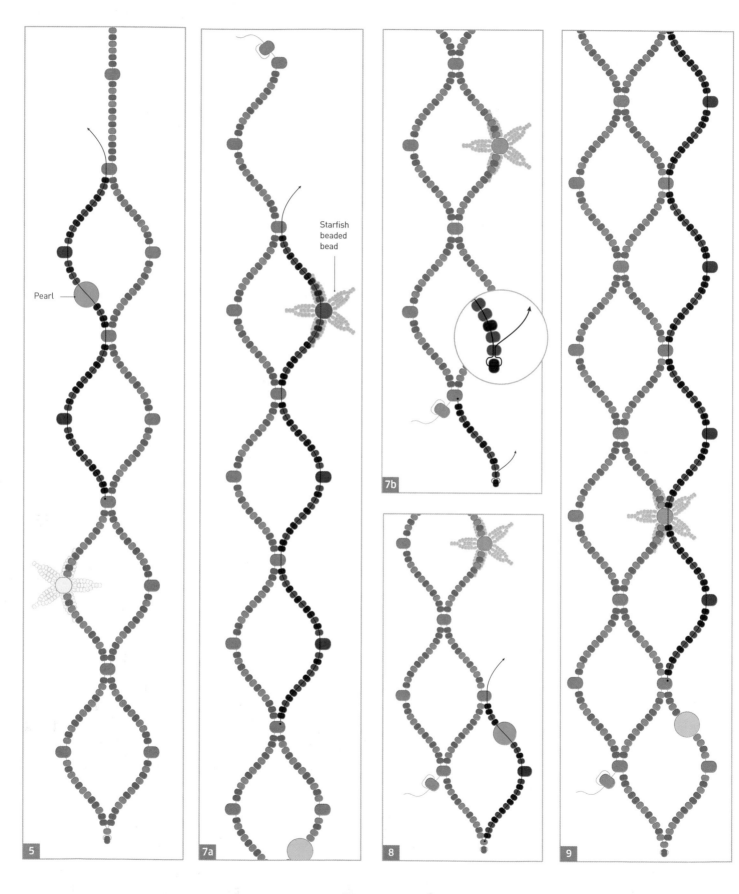

Pearl

Starfish beaded bead

5

7a

7b

8

9

5 Pick up 4 seed beads, 1 pearl, 4 seed beads, 1 size 8, and 12 seed beads. Skip a size 8, and stitch through the next size 8 of the first row.

6 Add 22 plain nets with 1 size 8 at the center of each. Add 4 seed beads, 1 pearl, 4 seed beads, 1 size 8, and 12 seed beads.

7 Add 2 plain nets, 1 starfish net, and 1 plain net. Pass through the first size 8 added in step 2 (a). Flip the work vertically to continue stitching from left to right. Pick up 14 seed beads, and pass back through the thirteenth bead added (b).

8 Pick up 12 seed beads, 1 size 8, 4 seed beads, 1 pearl, and 4 seed beads. Skip 1 size 8, and stitch through the following size 8 of the previous row.

9 Add 1 plain net, passing through the starfish added in the previous row, as you would for an 8 seed bead. Add 4 plain nets and 1 starfish net.

10 Add 18 plain nets. When the thread reaches about 10 in. (25 cm), add a new 2-yd (1.8-m) thread with a 12-in. (30-cm) tail, and weave in the old one before continuing.

11 Add 1 starfish net, 3 plain nets, and 1 pearl net. Finish the row with 14 seed beads.

12 Add 4 more rows of netting, with 1 starfish and 1 pearl placed randomly at each end, no higher than the starfish added in row 2. Space the accents and colors as evenly as possible. When passing through starfish beads for the second time, make sure that they are facing upward so that all starfish will be on the same side of the beadwork.

13 In the eighth row, add 1 pearl at each end. In the ninth row, add only plain nets with size 8 and 11 seed beads. Pass through the last size 8 bead at the end of row 8, then weave in all remaining thread and tails.

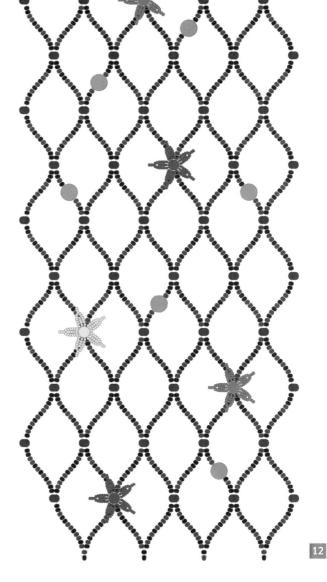

12

Place starfish and pearls evenly throughout the net.

Variations: To create a sunken treasure variation in your lariat, use a greater combination of seed beads in your mix, and add assorted glass, shell, or pearl accents to the ends. Try different combinations of aquatic colors, and make a matching Cyprus Sea Star Ring for a complete set (see page 79).

Securing your beadwork: To get an even dispersal of thread in the beadwork, weave old threads into the center rows, and weave tails in toward the edges.

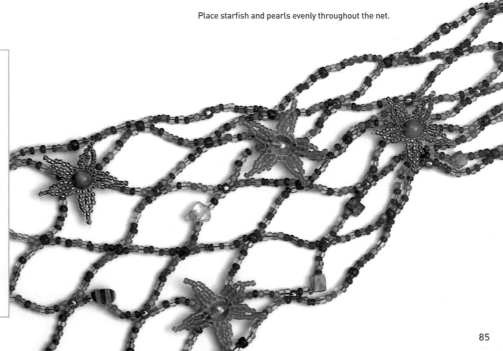

Red Stone Pendant

The Ancient Greeks loved their gemstones, and incorporated them into jewelry designs such as the necklace seen right. This medallion pendant project incorporates several shades of red with a hint of gold for a classical look. The negative space created by the peyote rings makes it light and airy, balancing the deep colors, and the clasp-free design is easy to wear.

TOOLS AND MATERIALS

- 14 yd (12.8 m) smoke braided beading line, 6 lb test (size D)
- Size 10 and 13 beading needles

Beads

- 4 g transparent garnet 8/0 Czech seed beads (1)
- 15 g transparent ruby 11/0 Czech seed beads (2)
- 8 g purple-lined hyacinth 11/0 Japanese seed beads (3)
- 4 g jet black 15/0 Japanese seed beads (4)
- 16 x 6.5 mm black Czech glass flat round coins (4)
- 26 x 5–6 mm gold freshwater semi-round pearls (5)

Dimensions: 27½ x 1½ in. (70 x 3.5 cm)

COLOR PALETTE

1	2	3
4	5	

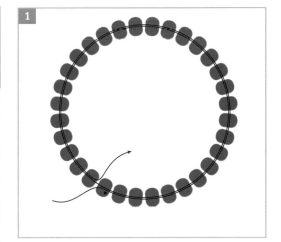

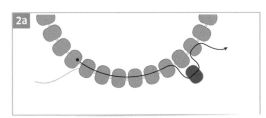

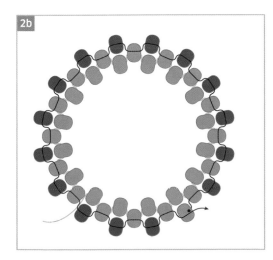

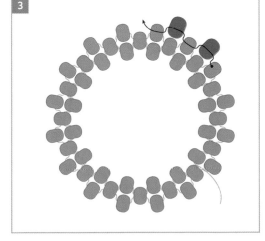

1 Thread a needle on 2 yd (1.8 m) of braided beading line. Pick up 32 black size 15 beads and slide them down to the end, leaving a 4-in. (10-cm) tail. Pass through all of the beads again to form a ring.

2 Stitch through the first 6 beads again. Pick up 1 black size 15 bead. Skipping the next bead in the ring, stitch through the following bead, and pull snug (a). Repeat around the ring to create the first round of circular peyote. Step up to begin the next round by stitching through the first bead added in this round (b).

3 Pick up 1 hyacinth size 11 bead. Stitch through the nearest raised black size 15 bead in the ring, and pull snug. Repeat around the ring, and step up through the first size 11 added in this round.

4 Work 1 more round in hyacinth size 11. Weave through the size 11 beads to secure the thread and trim.

5 Repeat to make 3 more rings with the remaining thread. Weave in the tails on each ring and trim, using your size 13 needle in tight spots if necessary. Make 4 additional rings with a new 2-yd (1.8-m) length of beading line, for a total of 8 small rings.

6 Thread a new 2-yd (1.8-m) length of beading line, and pick up 48 black size 15 beads. Pass through all of the beads again to form a ring, leaving a 6-in. (15-cm) tail.

7 Stitch through the first 6 beads again. Work 1 round of circular peyote with size 15 black beads, followed by 2 rounds of size 11 hyacinth. If your tension is very tight, the beadwork may begin to curve—gently stretch the ring back into shape and press flat at the end of each round as needed.

8 In the next round, add 1 size 11 hyacinth bead for the first stitch, followed by 1 size 8 garnet bead. Repeat for the entire round, and step up through the first size 11 added.

9 In the following row, add 1 size 8 garnet bead per stitch, and step up (a). For the final round, you will fill in the gaps between the size 8 beads. Step up through 3 size 8 beads, and add 1. Pass through the following 3 size 8 beads. Repeat around the ring (b). Weave in all remaining thread and trim. Repeat steps 6 through 9 to make a second medium ring.

10 To make the pendant ring, thread a needle on 2 yd (1.8 m) of beading line, and pick up 60 size 15 black seed beads. Pass through half of the beads again to form a ring, leaving a 6-in. (15-cm) tail. Work 1 round of circular peyote with size 15 black beads.

4
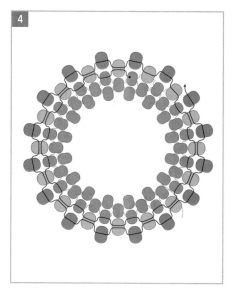

6-7
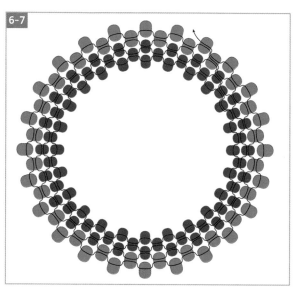

8
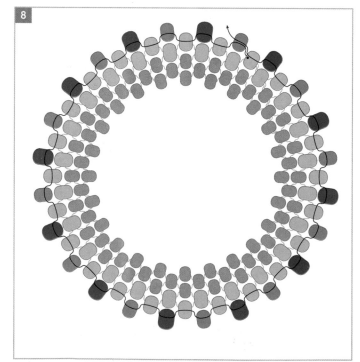

9a
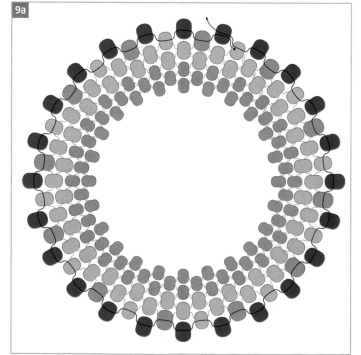

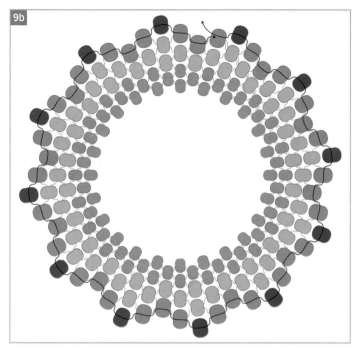

9b

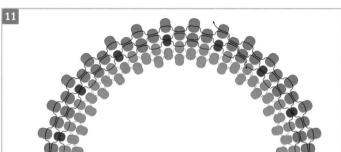

11

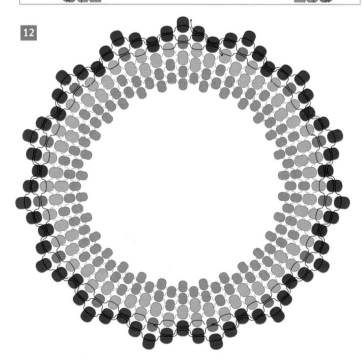

12

11 On the next round, add 1 size 11 hyacinth in the first stitch and 1 size 15 black bead in the second. Repeat around the ring, and step up. Work 2 rounds of size 11 hyacinth.

12 Work 1 round by alternating size 11 hyacinth and size 8 garnet beads. Step up, and add 1 round of size 8 garnet beads. In the final round of the ring, add 1 size 8 to each gap, stitching through 3 size 8 beads per stitch, as you did in step 9b. Weave in all thread and trim.

13 On a new 2-yd (1.8-m) length of beading line, pick up 60 size 11 ruby beads. Bring both thread ends together, and center the beads. Hold the threads together at the base of the beads to form a loop. From the top of the large peyote ring pendant, pass the loop through the center and under one edge. Pass both ends of the thread through the top of the loop, and gently pull snug to form a lark's head knot. Adjust the knot to make sure that it rests evenly around the peyote pendant with no slack and no threads are caught between the beads.

14 String 1 gold pearl onto the needle, and pass the other thread end through. Slide the pearl down to the bead knot. Set the thread end aside, and tape it to your workspace if desired.

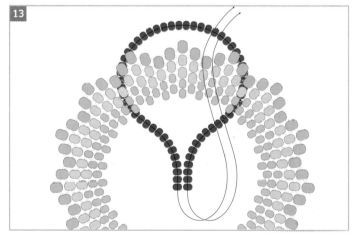

13

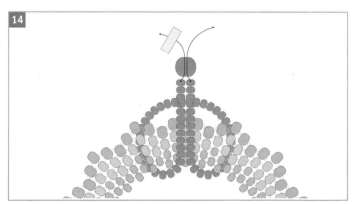

14

15

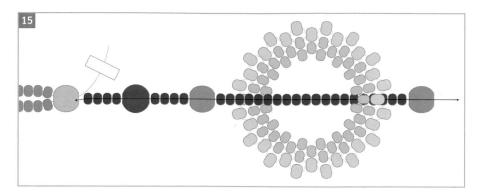

Stitch help: The small peyote rings will likely move around the bead strand as you work—stringing them in sequence helps make sure that none are left out before the second half of the chain begins. You can choose to string them on all at once if you prefer, then place them on the 20-bead sets as needed.

16

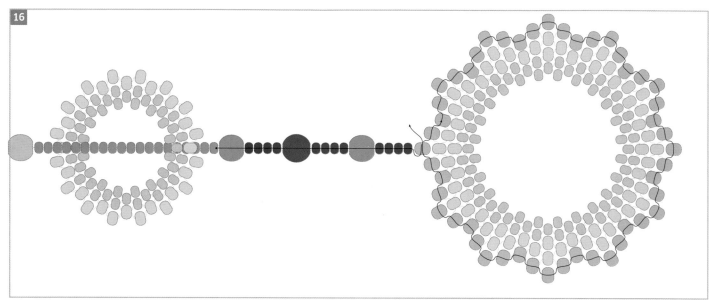

17

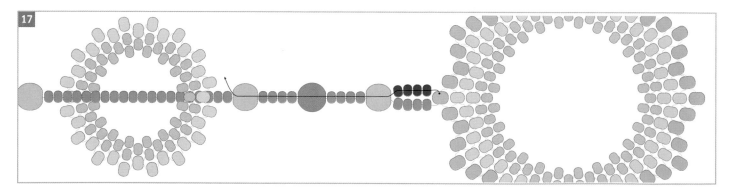

18

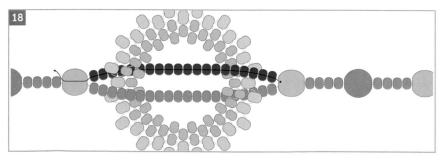

Variations: The semi-round pearl shapes give this necklace an ancient appeal, but the design looks just as beautiful with other shapes. Experiment with your favorite 6-mm glass and pearl accents to achieve different looks.

15 On the threaded needle, pick up 4 size 11 ruby, 1 black coin, 4 size 11 ruby, 1 pearl, and 20 ruby. Slide 1 of the small peyote rings over the beads and let it rest with the 20 ruby beads. Pick up 1 pearl, 4 ruby, 1 coin, 4 ruby, 1 pearl, 4 ruby, 1 coin, 4 ruby, 1 pearl, and 20 ruby. Slide on a small peyote ring.

16 Pick up 1 pearl, 4 ruby, 1 coin, 4 ruby, 1 pearl, and 4 ruby seed beads. Weave into 1 of the medium peyote rings, through a size 8 seed bead in the outermost round. Pass through all of the size 8 seed beads around the edge of the ring, exiting from the first one entered.

17 Pick up 4 ruby beads, pass through the last pearl added in the previous step, and pull snug. Continue weaving through the beads in the strand, exiting from the next pearl, just before the first set of 20 ruby beads.

18 Lay the nearest small peyote ring across the strand, with the 20 ruby beads passing over and under the ring. Pick up 20 new size 11 ruby, and pass them under and over the ring. Stitch through the next pearl, and pull snug to capture the ring between the two strands.

19 Pass through the beads in the strand, and exit from the pearl before the next set of 20 ruby. Repeat step 18 to capture the next small ring. Stitch through the remaining beads in the strand, and remove the needle from the thread for now.

20 Repeat steps 15 to 19 with the other half of the thread, securing a new chain to the second medium ring and weaving the small rings into the chain. Weave in both threads and trim.

21 Attach a stop bead to a new 2-yd (1.8-m) length of thread, leaving an 8-in. (20-cm) tail. Weave into 1 of the medium peyote rings, and exit from a size 8 bead directly opposite from the chain that was just added.

22 Pick up 4 size 11 ruby, 1 pearl, 4 ruby, 1 coin, 4 ruby, 1 pearl, and 20 ruby beads. Slide on 1 small ring. Add 1 pearl, 4 ruby, 1 coin, 4 ruby, 1 pearl, 4 ruby, 1 coin, 4 ruby, 1 pearl, and 20 ruby. Slide on another small ring.

23 Pick up 1 pearl, 4 ruby, 1 coin, and 4 ruby. Add 1 pearl, and repeat the entire pattern in reverse, including the last 2 small rings. Weave into the other medium peyote ring through the size 8 directly across from the existing chain. Pass through all of the size 8 beads on the edge of the ring and exit from the first again.

24 Pick up 4 size 11 ruby beads, and pass through the last pearl added in the chain. Pull snug. Weave through the following beads, and exit from the pearl before the next set of 20 ruby beads. Pick up 20 size 11 ruby, and pass through the small peyote ring to capture it. Repeat to the end of the chain, securing the remaining rings.

25 Pass through the first pearl added to the chain. Pick up 4 size 11 ruby beads, and pass through the size 8 seed bead in the medium ring, where the chain began. Weave around the edge of the ring, weave any remaining thread into the chain, and trim.

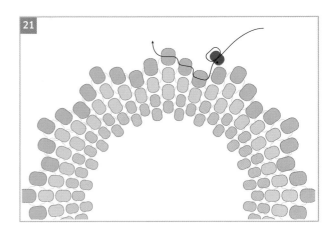

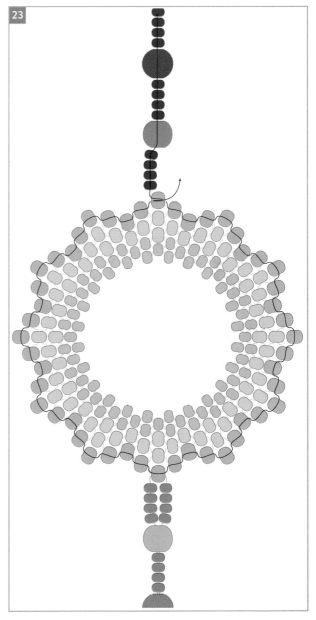

The classical civilization of Ancient Rome began as the Roman Kingdom around 800 BCE, followed 300 years later by the Roman Republic. The Roman Empire was established by Augustus in 27 BCE, and endured until the end of the fifth century CE. By that time, the empire spanned much of Europe and regions surrounding the Mediterranean, with colonies reaching as far as Britain and North Africa.

Jewelry in Ancient Rome was created with a wide variety of materials, made available by trade routes throughout the enormous empire. Gemstones like carnelian, jasper, and lapis lazuli from Persia were popular, as were pearls from the Persian Gulf. The Romans also imported emeralds from Egypt and amber from the Baltics.

CHAPTER 3 ◼
Ancient

Many popular jewelry designs in Ancient Rome were inspired by Greek and Etruscan styles. Rings were the most popular jewelry worn by elite men, while women usually enjoyed a variety of adornments. In addition to gold bangles and intricately carved gemstone earrings, the Romans favored functional jewelry such as brooches and fibula—decorative pins for fastening clothing.

In this chapter, we'll explore classic Roman motifs and jewelry styles, while incorporating modern variations of beads found in Ancient Roman jewelry. Seed bead palettes and beadweaving techniques combine to honor some of the most inspiring goddesses in the Roman pantheon, as well as everyday items used across the empire.

Rome

Roman-Glass Necklace

At its peak, the Roman Empire was massive, stretching across the known world. Today the remnants of Ancient Roman settlements provide a unique glimpse into another time. One settlement in Afghanistan is a treasure trove of old Roman glassworks, which produced vessels such as the one shown left. This necklace is inspired by Ancient Roman necklaces, with a multitude of coin-shaped dangles made from genuine Ancient Roman glass—making a necklace that reaches back through history.

SKILL LEVEL: **BEGINNER**
TECHNIQUES: **DAISY CHAIN VARIATION, STRINGING**

TOOLS AND MATERIALS

- 6 yd (5.5 m) crystal braided beading line, 6 lb test (size D)
- Size 10 beading needle

Beads
- 8 center-drilled Ancient Roman glass disks (1)
- 28 x 6 mm topaz AB glass druks (2)
- 30 x 5 mm turquoise green wood heishi (3)
- 44 x 5 mm black wood heishi (4)
- 56 x rootbeer AB 8/0 seed beads (5)
- 8 g medium topaz 11/0 seed beads (6)

Dimensions: 21 x 1⅓ in. (54 cm x 3.5 cm)

COLOR PALETTE

1	2	3
4	5	6

1 Choose one Roman glass disk that is 18–20 mm in diameter, and set aside. Arrange the remaining 7 disks by color, shape, or size, until you have a pattern that you like.

2 Attach a stop bead to 1 yd (0.9 m) of beading line, leaving a 4-in. (10-cm) tail. Pick up 13 size 11 seed beads, and stitch back through the first 2 beads again.

3 Pick up enough seed beads to span the radius of your first disk, from the outside edge to the hole, plus 2 more seed beads. String the disk and the same number of seed beads again. Adjust the quantities if necessary to achieve a nicely draped dangle.

4 Stitch up through the same 2 beads from step 2 and pull snug. Pass through all of the beads twice, tie a half-hitch knot between two beads (Techniques, page 131), and pass through a few more beads. Trim the thread.

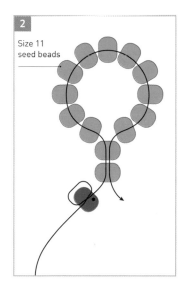

2
Size 11 seed beads

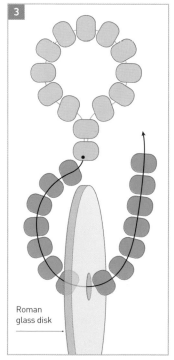

3
Roman glass disk

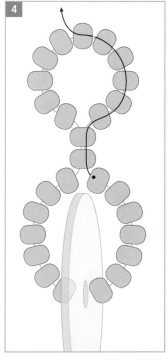

4

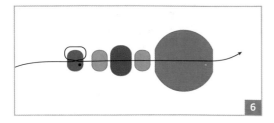

5 Repeat for the other 6 disks using the remaining thread to make a total of 7 glass dangles. Weave in the ends and trim the tails.

6 Attach a stop bead to 2 yd (1.8 m) of beading line, leaving an 8-in. (20-cm) tail. String on 1 size 11 seed bead, 1 size 8, 1 size 11, and 1 druk.

7 Pick up 7 size 11 seed beads and carefully stitch back up through the druk just added. Pull snug to form a loop of seed beads around the outside, making sure that the druk is snug against the base seed beads (a). Add 7 more seed beads to form a loop on the opposite side (b).

8 Repeat the pattern from step 6 to add 3 more druks with loops. String on 1 size 11, 1 size 8, 8 green heishi, 1 size 8, and a size 11. Add 4 druks with loops.

9 String on 1 size 11, 1 size 8, 1 green heishi, 3 black heishi, 1 size 8, and 1 glass dangle. Repeat the pattern in reverse, finishing with 2 druks.

10 Continue adding glass disks, following the same pattern of 8 heishi, followed by 2 druks with loops. Finish with 4 druks, 8 green heishi, and 4 more druks. Add new thread as needed.

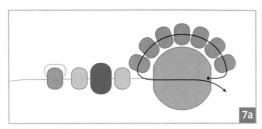

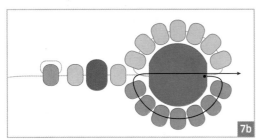

Repeat these patterns to create the necklace.

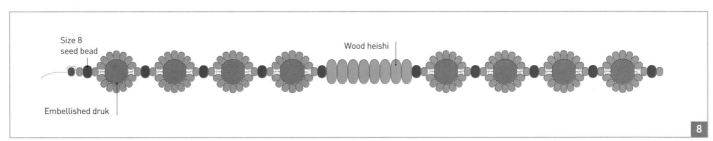

Size 8 seed bead

Wood heishi

Embellished druk

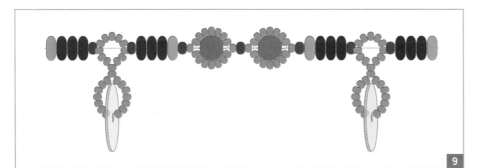

Securing your beadwork: When weaving in your threads and tails, pass through one 7-bead loop on every second druk, and knot each thread at least once.

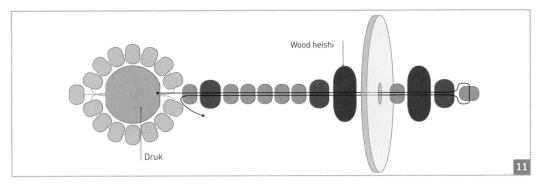

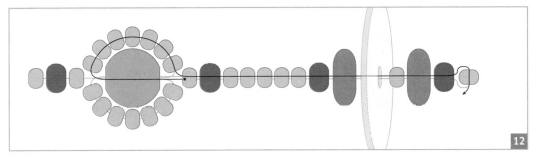

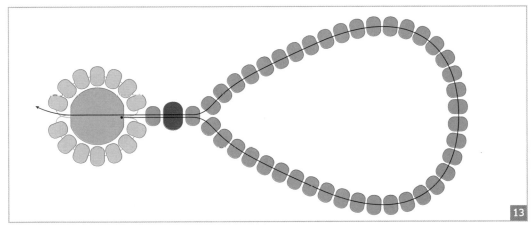

11 String on 1 size 11, 1 size 8, 5 size 11, 1 size 8, 1 black heishi, and the final glass disk. Add 1 size 11 bead that will fit securely into the disk hole, then add 1 black heishi, 1 size 8, and a size 11.

12 Skipping the last size 11 added, pass back through all of the beads again. Weave around the last druk in the chain, up through 1 of the seed bead loops, and pass through the clasp work twice more. Weave the remaining thread into the work and trim.

13 Remove the stop bead from the start of the chain. String on 40–44 size 11 seed beads to make a loop that will fit your glass disk button. Pass through the first bead added and through the following beads, exiting from the first druk. Pass through one of the 7-bead loops, then pass through the clasp loop again. Repeat for a second pass, then secure any remaining thread in the beadwork and trim.

Variations: The disk beads used in this necklace are made from glass excavated at Ancient Roman settlements in Afghanistan. Due to its age and rarity, Ancient Roman glass can be quite costly, and every strand is unique. For a more budget-friendly or uniform variation, substitute your favorite donut beads or recycled glass for the disks (see right).

Diana Earrings

The Roman goddess Diana represented hunting and fertility. In some versions of her myth, she was also a lunar and mother goddess—a lady of the moon. This project combines organic greens and moonlight whites in her honor. Circular shapes and dangles were a common motif in Roman earring designs like the pair shown left, making them easy to replicate with beads. This project uses just a few simple ingredients, which can be adapted to incorporate many patterns and accents to suit your taste.

SKILL LEVEL: **BEGINNER**
TECHNIQUES: **PEARL NETTING, STRINGING**

TOOLS AND MATERIALS

- 2 x 20-gauge 6 mm silver filled jump rings
- 2 x 21-gauge silver filled spiral earwires with rings
- 2 yd (1.8 m) crystal braided beading line, 6 lb test (size D)
- 64 in. (1.6 m) white nylon beading thread, size D
- Size 10 and 13 beading needles

Beads
- 24 x 4 mm white glass druks (1)
- 10 x 6 mm white glass druks (1)
- 6 g transparent dark green 11/0 seed beads (2)
- 2 g silver-lined gray 15/0 seed beads (3)
- 6 white 11/0 seed beads (1)

Dimensions: ⅔ x 3⅓ in. (1.5 x 8.5 cm)

COLOR PALETTE

1	2	3

1 Create two beaded beads using the braided line, druks, size 15, and dark green size 11 seed beads (Techniques, page 136).

2 Attach a stop bead to 32 in. (80 cm) of stretched, unwaxed nylon beading thread, leaving a 6-in. (15-cm) tail. String on 1 white 4 mm druk, 1 beaded bead, and 1 white 4 mm druk.

3 Pick up 27 green size 11 seed beads, 1 white 4 mm druk, and 1 white size 11. Skipping the white size 11, stitch back up through all of the beads again, exiting from the topmost druk.

4 Pick up 12 green size 11 and stitch back through the druk, beaded bead, and following druk.

5 Add 30 green size 11, 1 white 6 mm druk, and 1 white size 11. Skip the white size 11 and stitch back through all of the beads again, through the beaded bead, around the top loop, and through the druks and beaded bead.

6 Add 1 more fringe with 27 green seed beads and 1 white 4 mm druk. Weave in all remaining thread and the tail.

7 Open a jump ring. String on the top loop of the earring dangle and the earwire ring. Close the jump ring. Repeat to make a second matching earring.

2

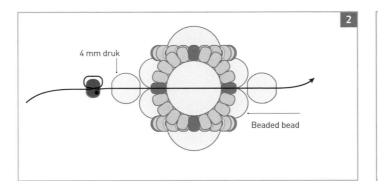

4 mm druk

Beaded bead

Matching sets: The simple materials make it easy to match these earrings to many other projects including the Perseus Pendant (page 54) and the Roman-Glass Necklace (page 94).

3

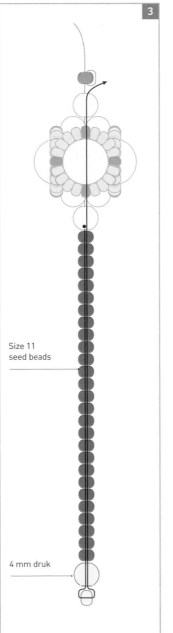

Size 11 seed beads

4 mm druk

4

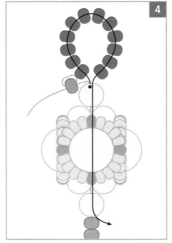

Variations: Create extra-long duster earrings by adding even more seed beads to each fringe. Remember to start with more thread to allow for the additional fringe length.

7

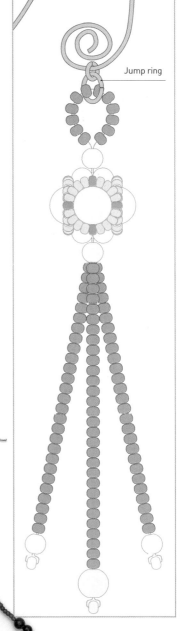

Jump ring

Eye of the Gods Ring

The subtle curves created by increasing and decreasing herringbone weave are ideal for making sensuous shapes in beadwork. This easy-to-stitch cocktail ring imitates the shape of the contoured eyes seen in Roman statues, like the one of Venus shown left. This project uses a peacock-eye palette for a mystical look. Tension is the key to bringing the eye shape together—once you've mastered it, you can make a set of eye rings to dazzle from every finger.

SKILL LEVEL: BEGINNER
TECHNIQUE: HERRINGBONE WEAVE

TOOLS AND MATERIALS

- 2 yd (1.8 m) smoke braided beading line, 6 lb test (size D)
- Size 10 beading needle
- Ring sizing mandrel or dowel

Beads
- 1 x 6.5 mm blue iris flat round coin bead (1)
- 3 g brown iris 11/0 seed beads (2)
- 3 g transparent lime 11/0 seed beads (3)

Dimensions: ⅓–½ in. (8–13 mm)

COLOR PALETTE

| 1 | 2 | 3 |

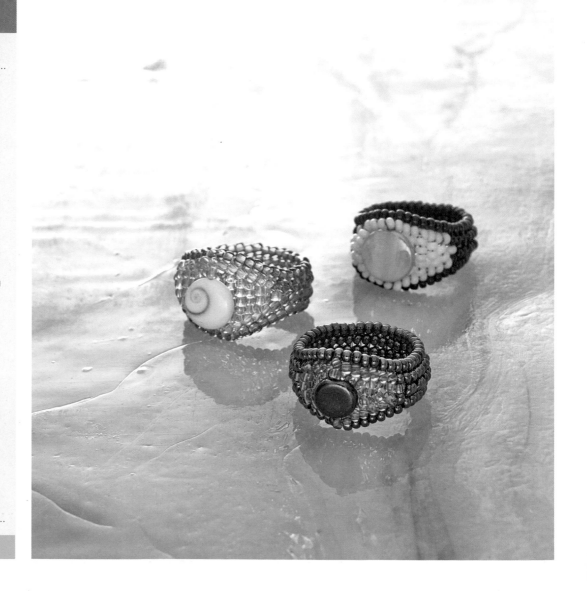

1 Thread a needle on 2 yd (1.8 m) of braided line. Leaving a 6-in. (15-cm) tail, use brown iris seed beads to stitch a 2-bead ladder that is 4 columns wide. Step up to begin a row of herringbone weave (Techniques, page 132).

2 Add rows of herringbone weave in brown iris seed beads until you have a strip that is about 1 in. (2.5 cm) long.

3 Step up to begin the next row. Pick up 1 brown and 1 green seed bead and stitch down through the next bead in the previous row as usual.

4 Pick up 1 green seed bead, then stitch up through the following bead in the next column.

5 Add 1 green and 1 brown bead for the final herringbone stitch in this row, then step up.

6 Add 1 brown and 1 green seed bead to start the next row. Stitch down through the previous row as usual.

7 Pick up 2 green seed beads and stitch up through the top bead of the next column. Add 1 green and 1 brown seed bead to finish the row.

8 Continue adding green seed beads to the center of the herringbone columns, increasing by one bead in each row until you have 6 green seed beads spanning the increase. Finish the row and step up.

9 Add 1 brown and 1 green seed bead to start the next row. Pass through the 6 green seed beads added to the increase in the previous row and up through the top green seed bead in the next column. Add 1 green and 1 brown seed bead to finish the row.

10 Step up and add 1 brown and 1 green seed bead to start the next row. In the increase, pick up 1 green seed bead, the blue iris flat glass bead, and 1 green seed bead. Stitch up through the top green bead of the next column. Pull the base of the thread snugly as you finish this row to secure the glass bead in the gap.

Shaping and sizing rings: The tapered shape of a ring mandrel allows you to easily size and stretch beaded rings. If you don't have one handy, you can use a wooden dowel, a marker pen, or other tubes around the house that roughly match the desired ring size. When using a dowel, stretch the ring carefully—if it becomes stuck, the beadwork may warp when working the ring free.

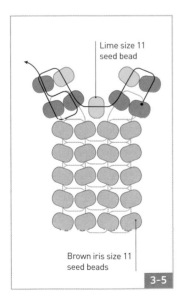

Lime size 11 seed bead

Brown iris size 11 seed beads

3–5

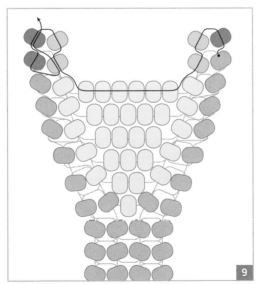

9

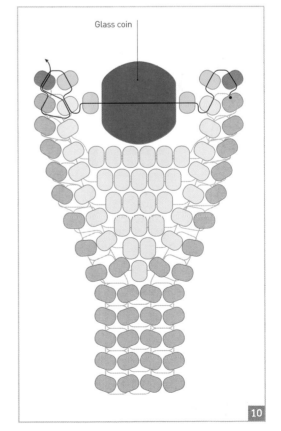

Glass coin

10

Variations: You can also use larger or smaller focal beads to get different looks. Round beads or coin shapes with a narrow edge fit snugly into the setting and will provide the most pleasing shapes.

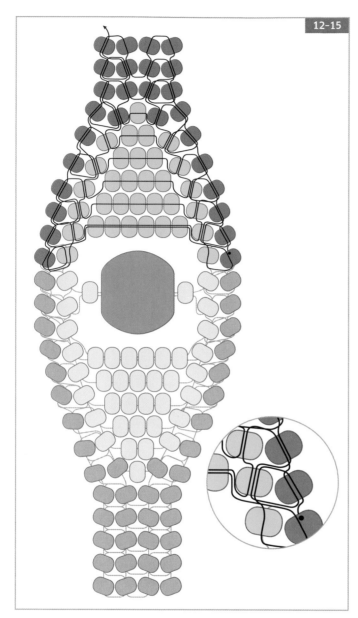

11 Finish the row with 1 green and 1 brown seed bead and step up. In the next row, add 1 brown and 1 green seed bead, then pass through the glass bead and 2 green seed beads in the increase and up through the top green seed bead in the next column. Finish the row and step up.

12 Add 1 brown and 1 green seed bead to start a new row. Pick up 7 green seed beads in the increase, and stitch up through the top green seed bead of the next column. Pull the base thread snug with each stitch to begin closing the gap around the glass bead, making sure it rests above the new set of 7 green seed beads.

13 Finish the row and step up. Continue adding new rows with herringbone, and decrease the green seed beads in the center by 1 with each stitch until you have 3 green beads in the gap.

14 For the remaining rows, pick up 2 brown seed beads for each herringbone stitch. Add 2 green seed beads to the increase and 1 in the following row.

15 Step up to add the next row and add 2 brown seed beads. Stitch up through the top bead in the following column, and pull snug to close the gap. Continue adding ordinary rows of herringbone weave in brown seed beads until the beadwork has reached the desired length for your ring.

Play with patterns:
You can create some interesting patterns by adding more colors to the beadwork. Divide the columns into two colors, or create a border around the increase by using a contrasting color for the beads added to the gap.

16 Test the fit of your ring on your finger or sizing mandrel. Thread a needle on the tail thread and stitch up through 5 or 6 beads to move the thread away from the edge.

17 Bring the ends of the beadwork together. Using the first needle, zip up the edges by weaving up and down through the first and last rows. Pull snug after every stitch to create a smooth join.

18 Weave the thread across the join twice, following the natural herringbone thread path. Weave the remaining thread through the ring, passing several times through the glass bead in the center and the outermost columns of the beadwork. Repeat with the tail thread and trim.

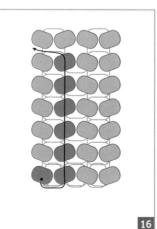

16

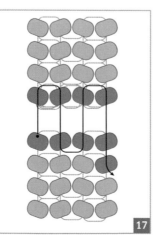

17

Amphora Cuff

The Romans borrowed much of their artistic inspiration from the Greeks, including pottery styles and motifs like the key pattern known as the "meander." This cuff is inspired by the classic black and gold artwork seen on ancient amphoras and urns like the one shown left, which were used to hold wine and olive oil. The slightly bulkier, more uniform shape of Japanese seed beads is ideal for making the pattern in this bracelet shine. Although it looks complex, the pattern repeats often, so once you've stitched a few rows, it is easy to refer to your beadwork for a reminder.

SKILL LEVEL: **INTERMEDIATE**
TECHNIQUES: **HERRINGBONE WEAVE, PEYOTE STITCH**

TOOLS AND MATERIALS

- 14 yd (13 m) smoke braided beading line, 6 lb test (size D)
- Size 10 beading needle

Beads

- 10 g jet black 11/0 Japanese seed beads (1)
- 10 g mustard yellow 11/0 Japanese seed beads (2)
- 10 g golden orange 11/0 Japanese seed beads (3)

Dimensions: 1 x 7 in. (2.5 x 17.8 cm)

COLOR PALETTE

1   2   3

1 Thread a needle on 2 yd (1.8 m) of beading line. Using black beads, stitch a 2-bead ladder with 14 columns, leaving a 12-in. (30-cm) tail (Techniques, page 132). Step up to begin a row of herringbone weave.

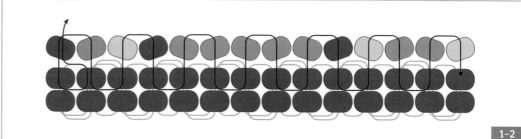

1-2

2 Add 6 rows of herringbone weave following the pattern shown using black, orange, and yellow seed beads. Repeat the pattern until the beadwork measures 5½ in. (14 cm) in length, or about 1 in. (2.5 cm) short of the desired length. Add new thread as needed, finishing the pattern with a row of 5 golden orange beads at the end of a key, as shown.

3 Add 2 rows of herringbone weave using black seed beads. Use the herringbone dummy stitch (Techniques, page 133) to secure the final two rows, and exit from the edge of the beadwork. Weave in any tails from thread that you've added, but leave the working thread and original tail.

4 Create a peyote toggle using 12 rows of black seed beads and finish with golden orange picots. (Techniques, page 134).

5 Pick up your working thread and string on 2 black seed beads. Skipping the second bead added, stitch through the first seed bead, and continue through the following 2 seed beads in the beadwork.

6 Stitch up through the 2 black seed beads of the next column. Repeat step 5 to add 5 additional fringes to the edge, stitching through the top row of beadwork only.

7 Add the sixth fringe and stitch up through the next column in the beadwork. Pick up 34 black seed beads to form a clasp loop. Stitch down through the top 2 beads of the next column and up through the following 2.

8 Add 6 more 2-bead fringes to the edge. Use any remaining thread to weave back through the clasp loop at least once, following the natural thread path, then secure the thread in the beadwork and trim.

9 Using your original tail thread, add 6 fringes to the opposite edge of the bracelet. On the seventh column, pick up 3 black seed beads, and weave through 2 beads at the center of the peyote toggle. Pick up 3 black seed beads, and stitch down through the top 2 beads of the next column.

10 Weave through the toggle stitch once more, and step up to add the remaining fringe.

11 Add 6 more 2-bead fringes to the edge of the bracelet. Weave in your remaining thread and trim.

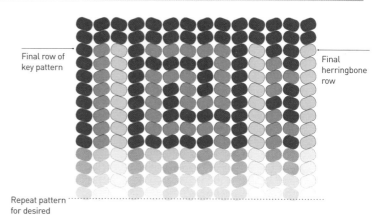

Final row of key pattern

Final herringbone row

Repeat pattern for desired length

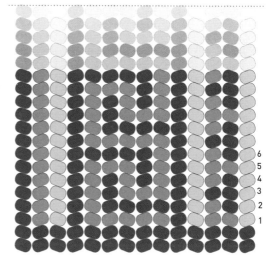

6
5
4
3
2
1

Color chart

Play with patterns: Although herringbone weave has a unique look, the beadwork is actually a simple grid, so this pattern can also be worked with square stitch, or on a loom. Try sketching out variations on graph paper and see where they take you.

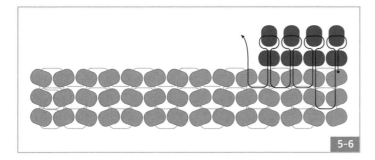

5-6

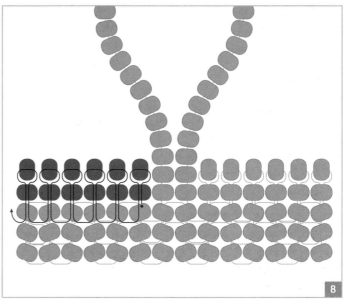

8

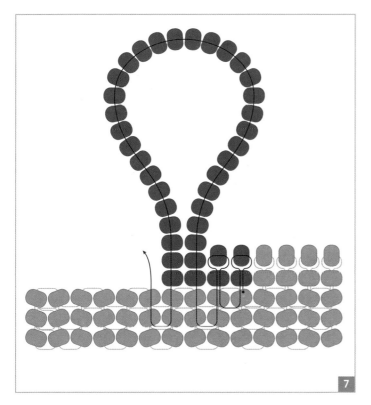

7

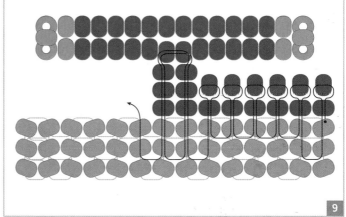

9

Variations: Experiment with different widths, create new borders, or double up on key patterns for a bold, classical look. The red and white variation is worked in square stitch, also using Japanese seed beads for a uniform shape.

Variations: If you can't find large-holed buri nut beads, round wooden macramé beads also work well. Another alternative is to use plain wooden beads, painted to match any palette you choose.

Etruscan Necklace

Much of Ancient Roman culture was inspired by the Etruscans (modern-day Tuscany), which was absorbed into the Roman Empire in the fourth century BCE. This project is inspired by actual Etruscan jewelry made from local materials, like the amber necklace shown left. Wooden beads are an excellent alternative to the large gemstones, allowing you to incorporate bold focals into the beadwork without adding a lot of weight. The natural colors and textures in this piece evoke an ancient aesthetic that is perfect for a boho wardrobe.

TOOLS AND MATERIALS

- 10 yd (9.1 m) black braided beading line, 6 lb test (size D)
- Clear nail polish
- Size 10 beading needle

Beads
- 56 x 3 mm metallic brown Java glass beads (1)
- 28 x 5 mm black striped Java glass beads (2)
- 24 x 6 mm black glass druks (3)
- 12 x 15 mm wood rondelles (4)
- 4 x 21 mm wood cone beads (4)
- 4 x 12 mm brown large-hole buri nuts (5)
- 4 x 12 mm black glass druks (3)
- 8 g brown iris 11/0 seed beads (6)
- 4 g transparent rootbeer 11/0 seed beads (7)
- 3 g black 8/0 seed beads (3)

- **Dimensions:** ¾ x 35 in. (2 x 90 cm)

COLOR PALETTE

1 String 1 buri nut on 1 yd (0.9 m) of braided beading line and stitch up through the bead again, leaving a 6-in. (15-cm) tail.

2 Pick up 13 size 11 rootbeer seed beads, and stitch back up through the nut bead again. Carefully pull snug to form a loop of seed beads on the outside (a). Add 12 rootbeer seed beads, and stitch up through the buri nut (b).

3 Repeat to add a total of 10 loops, alternating between 13 and 12 beads per stitch. Pass through all of the loops again, keeping the tension snug. Knot the thread between beads, weave in through 2 more loops, and trim.

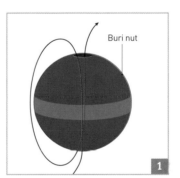

Buri nut

1

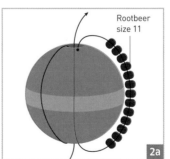

Rootbeer size 11

2a

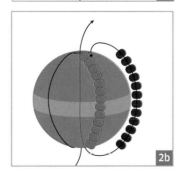

2b

Repeat this pattern 4 times to make the necklace.

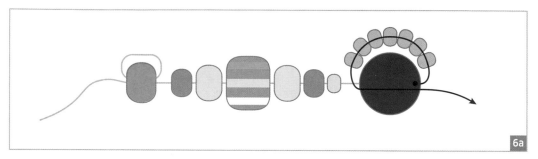

Beaded buri nut

Embellished druk

Java pattern

5-11

Size 8

3 mm Java   Size 11 brown iris

4

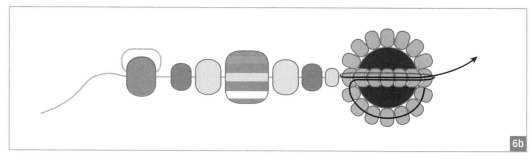

6a

6b

Variations: Java glass beads, made in Indonesia, have a wonderful organic quality that works well in ancient or tribal-inspired designs. If you can't get Java glass, substitute your favorite round beads, or use size 8 seed beads for the 3 mm Javas and size 6 seed beads for the 5 mm Javas.

4 Pull out the first stitch of tail thread, and weave it into the loops. Dab a little bit of nail polish onto the threads around the buri nut holes, being careful not to block them. Repeat steps 1–4 to embellish the remaining 3 beads, and allow to dry.

5 Attach a stop bead to 2 yd (1.8 m) of braided beading line, leaving a 10-in. (25-cm) tail. Pick up 1 size 8, 1 brown Java, 1 striped Java, 1 brown Java, and 1 size 8 seed bead. This basic pattern will be repeated throughout the chain. Add 1 brown iris size 11 seed bead and 1 black 6 mm druk.

6 Pick up 7 size 11 beads and stitch up through the druk (a). Pull snug to form a loop of seed beads around the outside, making sure that the druk is snug against the base beads. Repeat 3 more times to embellish the druk with 4 seed bead loops (b).

7 String on 1 brown iris size 11, your Java pattern, 1 size 11, and a 6 mm druk. Add 4 loops of 7 size 11 seed beads.

8 String on 1 brown iris size 11, the Java pattern, 1 beaded buri nut, 1 Java pattern, 1 size 11, and a 6 mm druk. Add 4 loops to the druk as usual.

9 String on 1 size 11 seed bead, 1 size 8, 1 wood rondelle, 1 size 8, 1 size 11, and a 6 mm druk. Add 4 seed bead loops to the druk.

10 String on 1 brown iris size 11, the Java pattern, a 12 mm druk, 1 Java pattern, 1 size 11, and a 6 mm druk. Add 4 seed bead loops to the druk.

11 String on 1 size 11 bead, 1 size 8, 1 wood rondelle, 1 size 8, 1 size 11, and a 6 mm druk. Add 4 seed bead loops to the druk.

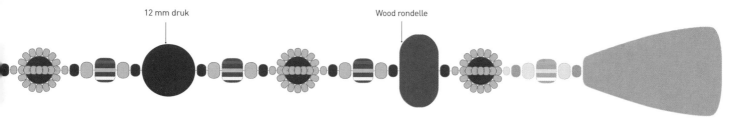

12 mm druk

Wood rondelle

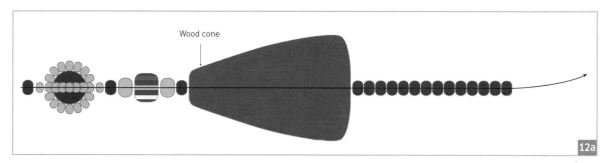

Wood cone

12a

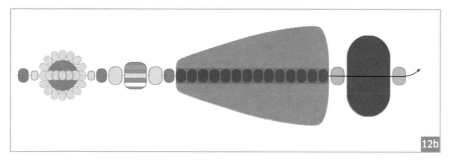

12b

12 String on 1 size 11, 1 Java pattern, and a wood cone. String on enough size 11 seed beads to fill the hole of the wood cone (a). String 1 size 8, 1 wood rondelle, 1 size 8, and a wood cone (b). Fill the new cone with seed beads.

13 Repeat the pattern in reverse, mirroring all of the beads added before the cone section, adding new thread as needed. Add a new wood rondelle, then begin the pattern again from step 5. Add the second set of wood cones and mirror the beaded section just added to complete the necklace chain.

14 Pick up 1 wood rondelle and pass through the first beads added to the chain to bring the ends together. Weave all remaining thread into the beadwork, passing through 1 seed bead loop on every druk. Tie at least one half-hitch knot (Techniques, page 131) between beads with each thread.

Securing your beadwork: Weaving thread in between the wooden cone sections can be a tight fit. Use a fresh beading needle if your usual needle has become curved with use, and carefully push the eye of the needle up to the last seed bead until the tip passes through the cone. If necessary, you can use a pair of round-nose pliers to pull gently on the tip of the needle to finish the pass.

Play with patterns: This necklace is long enough to slip over the head, and requires no clasp; you can wear it with the cones to the sides, or front and back. To make a shorter variation with a single set of cone beads at the center, work steps 5 to 13 but do not repeat, then finish the ends with a button and loop clasp.

Toga Multistrand Pendant

One of the most familiar images of the Ancient Roman world is the toga, modeled here by the Goddess of Abundance statue in Piazza del Popolo, Rome. This simple but elegant garment worn by both men and women provided a fantastic backdrop to showcase gorgeous jewelry. With this necklace, you can capture the look of a flowing white robe and a lovely heirloom all in one. Deceptively simple chains of right-angle weave (RAW) mimic the look of both metal chains and draped linen in this multistrand piece. Single rows of right-angle weave work up quickly in shades of white with just a hint of gold, and are finished with a beautiful carved bone pendant.

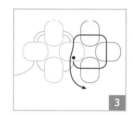
2

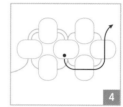
3

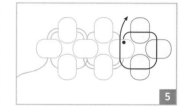
4

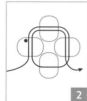
5

SKILL LEVEL: INTERMEDIATE
TECHNIQUE: RIGHT-ANGLE
WEAVE (RAW)

TOOLS AND MATERIALS

- 10 yd (9.1 m) crystal braided beading line, 6 lb test (size D)
- Size 10 beading needle

Beads
- 1 carved bone infinity pendant (1)
- 3 opaque white 6 mm glass druks (2)
- 4 opaque white 8/0 seed beads (2)
- 4 g opaque white 11/0 seed beads (2)
- 4 g pearl white 11/0 seed beads (3)
- 4 g pearl light cream 11/0 seed beads (4)

Dimensions: 21½ in. (55 cm)

COLOR PALETTE

1	2
3	4

1 Thread a needle on 2 yd (1.8 m) of braided beading line. Pick up 4 size 11 opaque white seed beads, and slide them down to the end of the thread, leaving an 8-in. (20-cm) tail.

2 Stitch through the first 2 beads added again, and pull the thread snug to form a cluster. Continue through the third bead, and pull snug to complete the first RAW stitch.

3 Pick up 3 opaque white seed beads. Stitch through the third bead from the first step again, following the thread. Pull snug.

4 Stitch through the first 2 beads added in step 3. Pull the thread tight to form a new RAW cluster.

5 Pick up 3 opaque white seed beads and stitch through the second bead added in step 3, following the thread. Pull snug.

6 Continue adding 3 beads at a time with RAW until you have a chain that is 16½ in. (42 cm) long, adding a new 2-yd (1.8-m) length of thread when needed. Weave in the tail from the newly added thread, but leave the tails at each end of the chain.

7 Repeat steps 1 to 6 to create 2 more chains—one in pearl white and one in light cream. Weave in new threads but leave the first and last tail.

8 Attach a stop bead to 1 yd (0.9 m) of braided beading line, leaving a 6-in. (15-cm) tail. Pick up 60 light cream seed beads, and slide them down to the stop bead.

Variations: Infinity pendants are available in a range of materials and styles, and the carved bone variety can be very elaborate. Shop around for one that suits your personal style.

9 String the top of the bone pendant over the seed beads, then pass the needle through the opening again. Stitch through the first 4 beads added in step 2 and carefully pull snug to form a double loop of seed beads at the top of the pendant.

10 Pass through all of the seed beads again, moving a few beads at a time and pulling the thread snug with each stitch. Repeat to strengthen the bail, tying 3 half-hitch knots between beads as you move through the loops (Techniques, page 131). Stitch through a few more beads to secure the thread, and trim.

11 Create a button clasp using a white druk bead (Techniques, page 137). Include three rounds of pearl white and a picot finish in light cream (Techniques, page 138).

12 Thread a needle at one end of the white chain. Pick up 1 opaque white size 8, 1 druk, and 1 opaque white size 8. Slide them down to the chain.

13 Pick up 45 pearl light cream seed beads. Stitch down through the first 3 beads picked up, and then continue through the size 8 beads and druk. Pull the thread snug to form a clasp loop.

14 Weave into the topmost bead of the RAW chain, from the opposite side that the thread was exiting in step 5, so that both sides of the bead are connected to the clasp area. Weave through the next 2 seed beads in the chain and pull snug.

15 Weave the remaining thread into the chain, following the natural thread path. Circle back

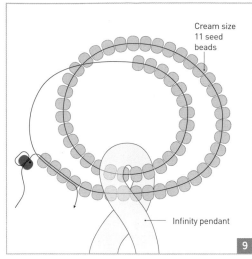

Cream size 11 seed beads

Infinity pendant

9

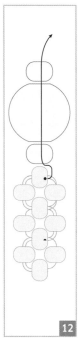

12

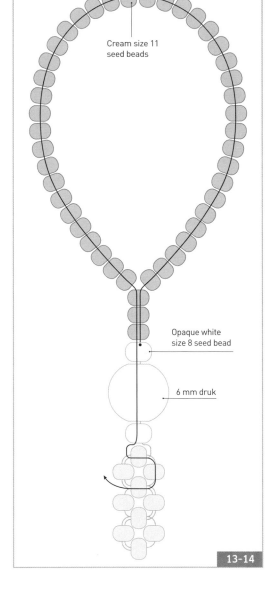

Cream size 11 seed beads

Opaque white size 8 seed bead

6 mm druk

13-14

toward the clasp area when the thread gets low, then trim the thread as close to the beads as possible.

16 Thread a needle on the pearl white chain, and carefully weave through the size 8 seed beads and druk. Pass through all of the beads in the clasp loop and back down through the druk area again.

17 Press the two RAW chains flat against each other, then stitch through the topmost bead of the pearl white chain. Pull snug to secure the position of the chains, then weave in the remaining thread.

18 Thread a needle on the pearl light cream chain. Holding the first two chains together, stitch into the druk area from one side, setting the third chain perpendicular to the other 2. Pass through all of the beads in the clasp and back down into the chain as before. Weave in the remaining thread.

19 Thread a needle on the tail thread of the opaque white chain. Pick up 1 opaque white

size 8 bead, 1 druk, 1 opaque white size 8 bead, and 10 light cream seed beads, and stitch though the druk of the button.

20 Add 7 pearl light cream seed beads, and stitch back down through the first 3 beads added in step 12. Pull snug to form the clasp.

21 Stitch down through the size 8 seed beads and druk, and

weave through the topmost bead of the RAW chain. Weave in the remaining thread and trim.

22 Lay your necklace out straight on your work surface. When securing the final 2 chains to the button clasp, make sure that the strands are not overlapping or twisted. Thread a needle on the pearl white chain, and lay it flat against the opaque white chain.

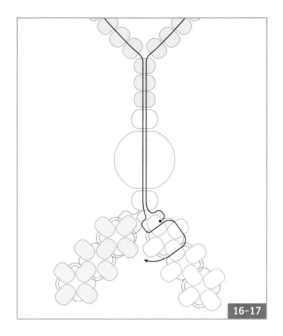

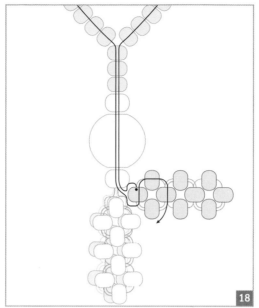

Stitch help: To get the right-angle weave chains really even and uniform, pull your thread tight after every needle movement. Firm, even tension will pull all of the beads into place for a beautiful chain.

23 Stitch through all of the beads in the clasp area and then back down into the chain to weave in the thread.

24 Thread a needle on the light cream chain and stitch into the druk area between the two previous chains. Weave through the clasp area and back down through the topmost bead of the light cream chain. Stitch up through the clasp beads once more for added strength, then weave in the remaining thread and trim.

25 Pass the loop clasp end of the chains through the double loop bail of the infinity pendant, and the necklace is complete.

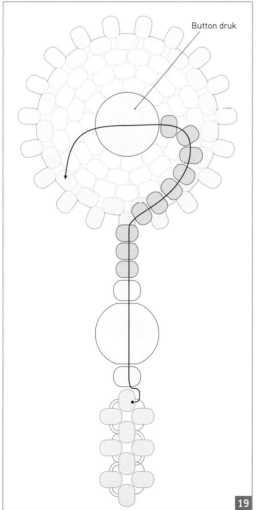

Button druk

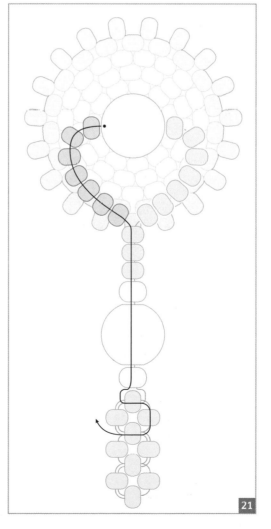

TOGA MULTISTRAND PENDANT

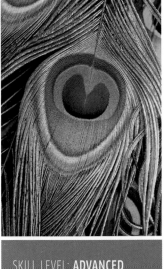

Juno Necklace

Juno was the wife of the chief Roman god Jupiter—the queen of the gods and protector of Rome. She was a goddess of marriage and childbirth and represented vitality and life. Her symbol was the peacock, whose feathers are still associated with royalty and divinity. The shape of this design is inspired by medallion jewelry from Roman Alexandria. Several classic beadwork stitches are combined to create this necklace. Though the final construction is simple, the overall effect is stunning. When you wear it, you'll feel like the queen of the gods.

SKILL LEVEL: ADVANCED
TECHNIQUES: SPIRAL ROPE, PEYOTE STITCH, STRINGING

TOOLS AND MATERIALS

- 12 yd (11 m) smoke braided beading line, 6 lb test (size D)

Beads

- 1 x 1½ in. (38 mm) green crystal donut pendant [1]
- 9 forest green freshwater baroque pearls [2]
- 1 x 6 mm black glass druk [3]
- 12 g transparent brown 11/0 seed beads [4]
- 5 g transparent sea blue 11/0 seed beads [5]
- 5 g black 11/0 seed beads [3]

Dimensions: 18 x 4 in. (46 x 10 cm)

COLOR PALETTE

1	2	3
4	5	

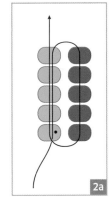

2a

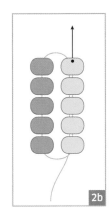

2b

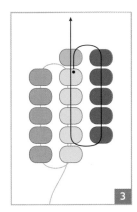

3

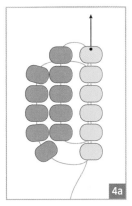

4a

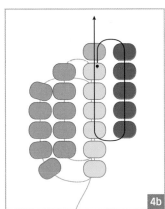

4b

1 Thread a needle on 2 yd (1.8 m) of braided line. Pick up 5 blue seed beads and 5 brown seed beads. Slide them down to the end of the thread, leaving a 10-in. (25-cm) tail.

2 Stitch up through the 5 blue seed beads and pull snug (a). Place the brown beads to the left of your needle and working thread before continuing (b).

3 Pick up 1 blue seed bead and 5 brown seed beads. Stitch up through the top 4 beads from the previous stitch. Pull snug, and stitch up through the blue bead just added.

4 Keeping the brown beads from each new row to your left as you work (a), repeat step 3 until you have a spiral rope that is 16 in. (41 cm) long, adding new thread when needed (b). Weave in the tails from any new threads, but leave your working thread and original tail.

5 Create a beaded button using your 6 mm black druk (Techniques, page 138). Include 1 round of blue seed beads, 2 rounds of brown, and finish with a picot edge in brown (Techniques, page 138).

Variations: Adding the pendant and pearls separately allows this necklace to be made with nearly any rope stitch.

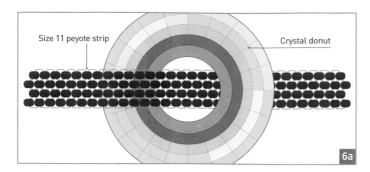

Size 11 peyote strip

Crystal donut

6a

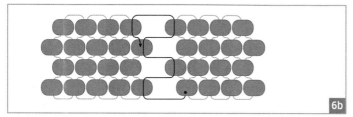

6b

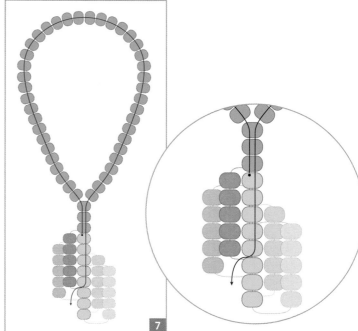

7

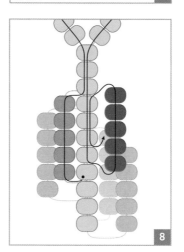

8

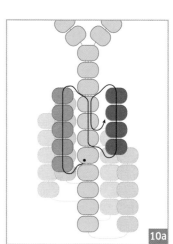

10a

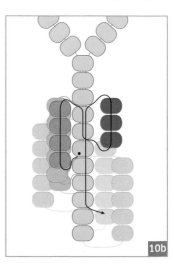

10b

6 Using 1 yd (0.9 m) of beading line and all black seed beads, create a strip of peyote stitch that is 4 rows wide and 2 in. (5 cm) long. Weave in the tail thread. Pass one end of the strip through the crystal donut (a), then zip up the edges and weave in all remaining thread (b), (Techniques, page 134).

7 Pick up the thread from your spiral rope again. Add 45 blue seed beads to make a clasp loop. Stitch back through the first 3 beads just added, and then continue through the top 5 blue beads in the spiral rope core.

8 Test the fit of your loop against your beaded button, adjusting the length if necessary, then weave through the loop once more, stitching up through the last row of brown seed beads added to the spiral to reverse the direction of the thread. Exit from the fourth bead at the top of the spiral core.

9 Pick up 5 brown seed beads and stitch down through the top 3 blue beads in the core, exiting from the open area, away from the existing spirals. Pull snug.

10 Pick up 4 brown beads and stitch down through the top 2 blue beads in the core (a). Pick up 3 brown beads and stitch through several blue beads in the spiral core, then weave in any remaining thread (b).

11 With the first tail thread, pick up 9 blue seed beads, pass through the druk at the back of the button, and pick up 6 blue seed beads. Stitch down through the first 3 blue beads just added, and through the top 5 blue beads in the spiral core.

12 Weave through the button stitches twice, then taper the end of the spiral following steps 9 and 10.

13 Pass the loop end of the rope through the peyote stitch ring to string on the crystal pendant. Secure the button clasp, then center the pendant on the rope.

14 Arrange the freshwater pearls on your work surface by size and shape, with the largest in the center, and similar shapes or sizes opposite each other for a symmetrical pattern.

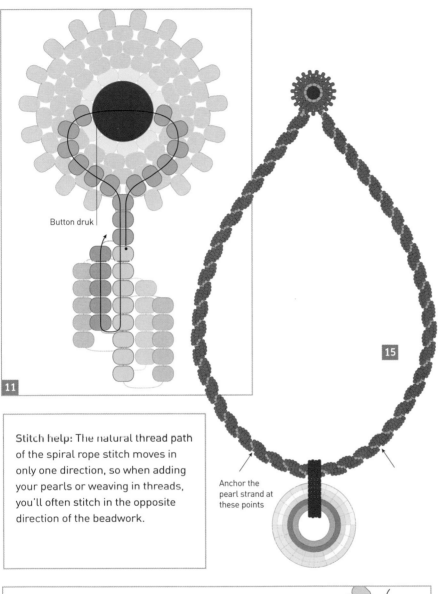

Button druk

11

Stitch help: The natural thread path of the spiral rope stitch moves in only one direction, so when adding your pearls or weaving in threads, you'll often stitch in the opposite direction of the beadwork.

15 Attach a stop bead to 1 yd (0.9 m) of braided line, leaving a 6-in. (15-cm) tail. Count up 4 spirals from the pendant and enter the beadwork through 2 beads in the blue spiral core, moving toward the pendant from the outside of the rope.

16 Pick up 10 black seed beads and 1 pearl. Repeat this pattern, stringing on all of the pearls in order, and finish with 10 black seed beads.

17 Stitch up through 2 blue beads in the spiral core, directly opposite from your start point on the other side of the pendant.

18 Weave through 4 more core beads and up into a brown row. Pass through 2 blue beads, moving back toward the pendant and through the closest row of brown beads. Weave through the blue core beads and back into the black seed bead strand. Pass through the strand and weave around the rope at least once more to strengthen, then weave any remaining thread into the rope.

19 Remove the stop bead from the tail thread, repeat step 18 to secure the thread, and trim.

15

Anchor the pearl strand at these points

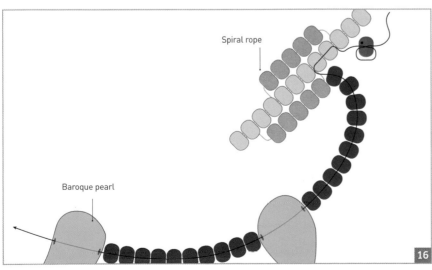

Spiral rope

Baroque pearl

16

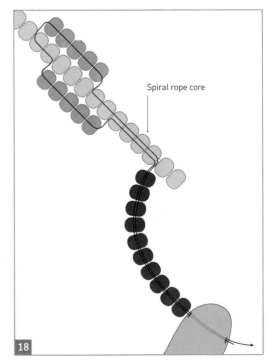

Spiral rope core

18

Variations: The size 8 seed bead cuff base leaves lots of room to experiment with embellishments. Add as many or as few coins as you like, decorate with stitches such as daisy chain, or add extra fringe for a wonderfully organic bracelet.

Earth Mother Cuff

Many ancient cultures had legends of an earth mother. In Ancient Rome, she was Terra Mater, or Tellus—the embodiment of flowers, fruit, and crop staples such as olives. The name Tellus was synonymous with "earth" or "ground." This earthy project is inspired in part by classic Roman coin bracelets, but it is a beadweaver's delight. Using size 8 seed beads for the base creates a wonderfully supple cuff that is easy to decorate, and the edge trim is built in for even faster weaving.

SKILL LEVEL: **ADVANCED**
TECHNIQUES: **PEYOTE STITCH, EMBELLISHING**

TOOLS AND MATERIALS

- 12 yd (11 m) smoke braided beading line, 6 lb test (size D)
- Size 10 beading needle

Beads

- 1 Czech glass button with metal shank (1)
- 3 Czech glass dragonfly coins (2)
- 30 g transparent brown rainbow 8/0 Japanese seed beads (3)
- 10 g transparent 3.4 mm Picasso drops (4)
- 8 g white-lined green 11/0 seed beads (5)

Dimensions: 1½ x 7 in. (3.8 x 18 cm)

COLOR PALETTE

1	2	3
4	5	

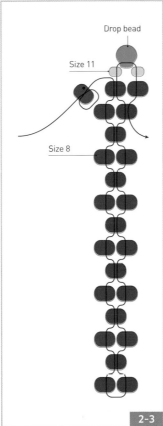

Drop bead

Size 11

Size 8

2-3

4

1 Thread a needle on 3 yd (2.7 m) of braided beading line. Attach a stop bead, leaving a tail 1 yd (0.9 m) long.

2 Pick up 14 size 8 seed beads and slide them down to the stop bead. Add 7 beads using peyote stitch and turn to begin the next row (Techniques, page 134).

3 Pick up 1 green size 11 seed bead, 1 drop, 1 size 11 green seed bead, and 1 size 8 seed bead. Stitch through the first raised bead from the previous row, and pull snug. Add 6 more size 8 beads with peyote stitch to finish the row.

4 To start the next row, pick up 1 size 11 seed bead, 1 drop, 1 size 11, and 1 size 8 bead. Finish the row with size 8 seed beads, as usual; pass through the second size 11 bead added in the previous row.

5 Pick up 1 drop, 1 size 11 seed bead, and 1 size 8 seed bead to start the next row. Finish with size 8 seed beads, and pass through the nearest size 11 bead at the edge. Repeat this step to create a peyote cuff base that is 5½ in. (14 cm) long, or about 1½ in. (4 cm) short of your desired length.

6 If you have less than 1 yd (0.9 m) of thread remaining, weave in and start a new 1-yd (0.9-m) thread, leaving a 6-in. (15-cm) tail. Add 2 rows of beadwork as usual to stabilize the new thread.

7 On the next row, add the trim and the following 2 size 8 beads. For the next stitch, pick up 1 size 11 seed bead, the button shank, and 1 size 11 seed bead. Stitch through the next raised bead as usual, and finish the row with size 8 seed beads.

8 Weave back through the row just added, treating the button and size 11 seed beads as one size 8. Weave through again to the end of the last row, and continue weaving as usual. Add 8 more rows of peyote stitch with trim, so that the beadwork extends just past the edge of the button.

9 Weave through the final 2 rows once to strengthen, then weave back through the beadwork, passing through the button row at least once more. Secure any remaining thread in the beadwork and trim.

10 Remove the stop bead from your first tail thread. Weave through the first 2 rows and exit from the first size 11 seed bead at the edge. Pick up 1 drop and 1 size 11 seed bead. Stitch down through the last size 8 bead on the edge, then weave through a few rows to secure the thread.

11 Exit from the second raised bead on the edge, facing outward. Pick up 30 size 8 seed beads. Counting back 3 raised beads from where your thread is exiting, pass through a raised bead on the opposite side of this edge, moving inward.

12 Weave through the clasp loop and peyote edge 3 times to strengthen. Weave in any remaining thread and trim.

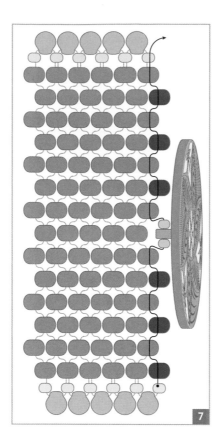

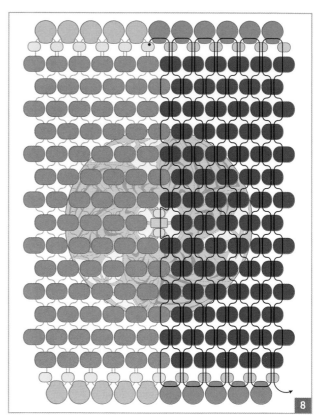

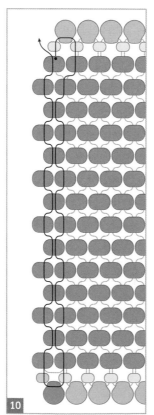

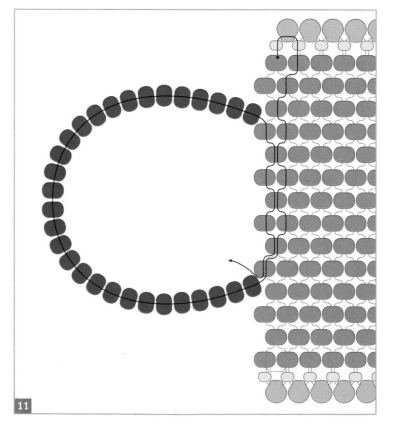

13

13 Thread a new 2-yd (1.8-m) length of beading line and attach a stop bead with a 6-in. (15-cm) tail. Ignoring the area covered by the button, center one dragonfly coin in the remaining beadwork.

14 From the underside of the beadwork, needle up between beads near the coin hole. Pass through the coin, and needle down between beads on the opposite side.

15 From the underside, weave across the beadwork, and needle through the space near the stop bead. Pass through the coin once more, and weave across a second time. Needle through the beadwork, and stitch through the coin once more, but do not needle through the cuff.

16 Pick up 1 size 8 seed bead, and stitch through the closest size 8 seed bead at the edge of the beadwork, nestling the new bead between two in the row below.

17 Weave around the edge and through the nearest 2 size 8 beads in the cuff. Pass through the coin, then repeat step 16 on this edge.

18 Weave around the edge, and pass back through the coin and the 2 raised size 8 beads once more. Secure the thread through several rows of beadwork and trim. Attach a new stop bead, and repeat to add 2 more coins, evenly spaced on either side. Weave in any remaining tails and trim.

16–17

Even a single coin looks earthy and elegant when embellished with assorted fringe.

Pompeii Bracelet

Long before the innovation of cultured pearls, the Romans treasured natural pearls for their beauty and rarity. Persian pearls were among the most luxurious materials available for jewelry making, appearing in many pieces like the necklace shown left. This project, inspired by a golden bracelet found at Pompeii, uses affordable freshwater pearls for just the right amount of shimmer. The two-needle technique, also known as the Russian chevron chain, provides a wonderful net to showcase these lovely beads.

TOOLS AND MATERIALS

- 2 yd (1.8 m) crystal braided beading line, 6lb test (Size D)
- 2 x size 10 beading needles

Beads

- 6 g buttercream size 11/0 seed beads (1)
- 20 x 6 mm top-drilled copper freshwater pearl coins (2)
- 11 x 6 mm tortoiseshell glass druks (3)
- 2 rootbeer size 8/0 seed beads (4)
- 1 x 18 mm Czech glass button (5)

Dimensions: 6½ x 1 in. (17 x 2.5 cm)

COLOR PALETTE

1	2	3
4	5	

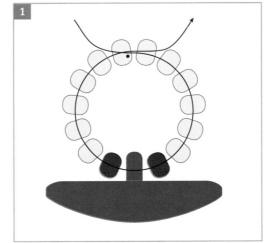

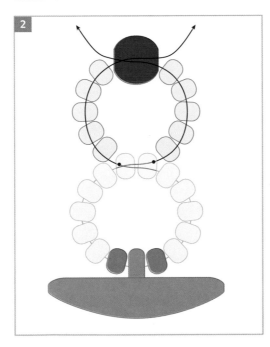

1 Thread a needle on 2 yd (1.8 m) of beading line and pick up 7 size 11 buttercream seed beads, 1 size 8 rootbeer, the Czech glass button shank, 1 size 8 rootbeer, and 5 size 11 buttercream seed beads. Center all of the beads on the thread and stitch back through the first 2 size 11 beads picked up. Pull snug to form a button loop, and make sure that the threads are even.

2 Add the second needle to the tail end of the thread. Pick up 5 size 11 buttercream beads and 1 druk. With the other needle, pick up 5 size 11 buttercream beads and pass through the druk in the opposite direction. Pull both threads snug.

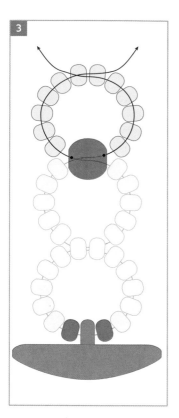

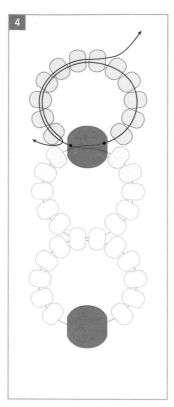

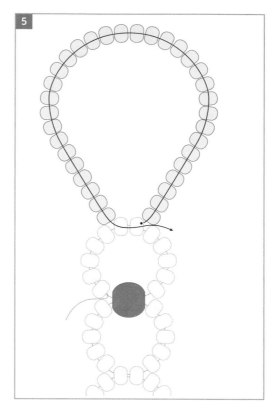

3 Pick up 7 buttercream size 11 seed beads. With the second needle, pick up 5 buttercream size 11 beads and pass through the first 2 seed beads just added to the opposite thread.

4 Repeat steps 2 and 3 until you have a chain with 11 druks, or until your chain is 1 in. (2.5 cm) short of the desired length. Add a final stitch as in step 3, but pass through all 7 beads picked up with the first needle. Remove the needle from this thread for now.

5 On the remaining needle, pick up 28 to 34 size 11 seed beads and stitch back through the center 2 beads of the loop created in the previous step. Test the fit of the loop on the button clasp and add or remove beads as needed.

6 Stitch through the following 5 beads in the chain, exiting next to the last druk. Turn the beadwork so that the button points away from you. Notice that each druk in the chain has 2 sets of 5 seed beads on each side. Pick up 1 size 11 bead, and stitch into the first 3 beads in the next set connected to this side of the druk.

7 Pick up 5 size 11 beads, 1 pearl, and 4 size 11 beads. Stitch up through the same bead that your thread is exiting and the following bead (the third and fourth beads in the set), and pull snug to form a rough loop. Stitch up through the first 3 seed beads just added.

8 Pick up 2 size 11 beads, and stitch up through the fourth and fifth beads in the next set of the chain. Pick up 1 size 11 bead, and stitch up through the first 3 beads of the next set in the chain.

9 Repeat steps 7 and 8 until you reach the end of the bracelet. After adding the eleventh pearl to this side of the chain, add 1 size 11 bead at the last druk in the chain, then weave around the button loop and through the opposite side of the chain. Pass through the first druk to park the thread, and remove the needle for now.

Stitch help: Working with two threads simultaneously can be tricky. To reduce tangles, place a pincushion at the center of your workspace. Pin each needle when you are not using it, and flip the beadwork as necessary to keep both threads straight.

10 Add a needle to the tail thread. Add chevrons and pearls to the other side of the chain as before, and weave around the button loop to exit from the opposite side. Weave in all remaining thread, passing through the sections where the chevrons connect to the chain, strengthening the beadwork.

6

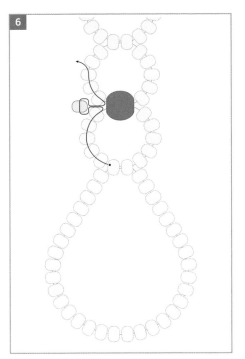

7

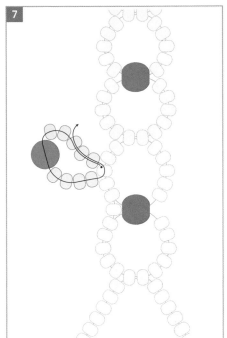

8

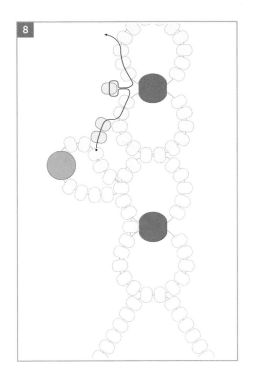

9

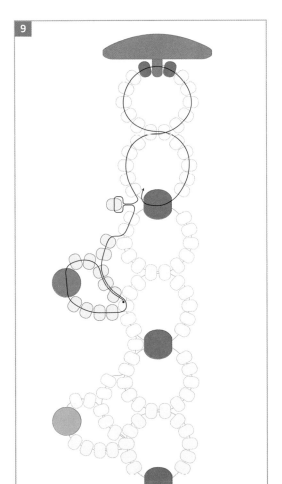

10

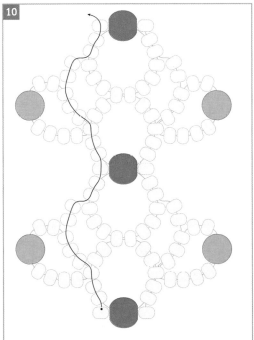

Weave in threads along the connections to strengthen the beadwork.

Variations: You can use a variety of pearl shapes or other accents in the chevron sections, though you may want to adjust the number of seed beads on either side to get a smooth fit. The first set of seed beads picked up in the accent loops should always be greater than the second set by one. If you replace the druks, be sure to use round beads that can turn freely—coins or other shapes will not rest evenly in the weave.

Bacchus Pendant

Bacchus was the Roman god of agriculture and wine, who traveled the world teaching people how to cultivate vineyards. To represent the most classical of beverages, this pendant takes the shape of a Roman amphora or wine jug. The gradual increase of bead sizes in a simple herringbone tube creates a pleasing shape. It also provides a great method for using up leftover beads from other projects.

SKILL LEVEL: **BEGINNER**
TECHNIQUE: **MODIFIED HERRINGBONE WEAVE**

TOOLS AND MATERIALS

- 32 in. (81 cm) black waxed cotton cord
- 2 yd (1.8 m) smoke braided beading line, 6lb test (size D)
- Size 10 beading needle

Beads

- 2 x 2.5 mm topaz O-shaped spacer beads (1)
- 2 g topaz 11/0 Japanese seed beads (1)
- 2 g transparent ruby 11/0 Czech seed beads (2)
- 12 transparent garnet 8/0 Czech seed beads (2)
- 12 rootbeer 8/0 AB Japanese seed beads (3)
- 12 x 3 mm red glass white-heart beads (4)
- 6 garnet Picasso 6/0 Japanese seed beads (5)

Dimensions: 2 x ½ in. (5 x 1.5 cm)

COLOR PALETTE

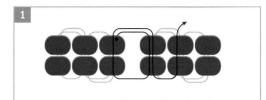

1

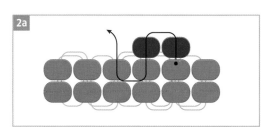

2a

2b

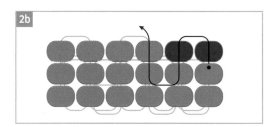

3

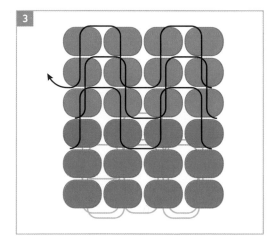

1 Thread a size 10 needle with 2 yd (1.8 m) of beading line and create a 2-bead ladder using size 11 ruby seed beads, leaving a 6-in. (15-cm) tail (Techniques, page 132). When you have a ladder that is 6 columns wide, weave the ends together into a ring (Techniques, page 133) and step up.

2 Pick up 2 size 11 ruby seed beads and stitch down through the top bead of the next column (a). Pull snug to form the first herringbone stitch of the round. Add two more pairs of ruby seed beads, then stitch up through the top 2 beads of the first column to step up (b).

3 Add on 3 rounds of herringbone weave using topaz size 11 seed beads, stepping up through 2 beads at the end of each round.

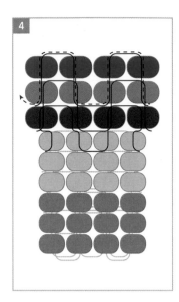

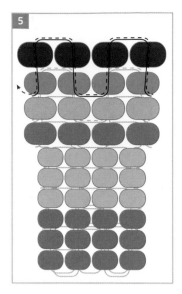

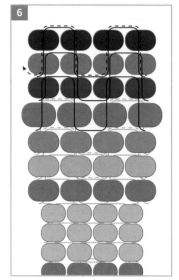

Bead selection: You can incorporate other seed bead shapes and 4-mm accent beads into this pendant for different looks. When making variations of this pendant, examine your bead choices carefully, and try to arrange them from smallest to largest. Sizes and shapes can vary slightly with every brand or batch.

4 Add 1 round of size 8 garnet beads, 1 round of size 8 rootbeer, and 1 round of white-heart beads. Tighten up the beadwork by doing a dummy stitch through the top 2 rounds just added: work 1 round of herringbone without picking up any beads, passing through the white-hearts and size 8 rootbeer beads in each column. Step up to exit from the white-heart in the first column.

5 Add 1 round of size 6 garnet beads and dummy stitch through the top 2 rounds again to tighten up any slack in the beadwork. Step up to begin the next round.

6 Add 1 round of white-heart beads, 1 round of size 8 rootbeer, and 1 round of size 8 garnet beads. Perform a dummy stitch at the end of every round.

7 After securing the size 8 garnet round, add 3 rounds of size 11 topaz, and 6 rounds of size 11 ruby seed beads (a). Dummy stitch the sixth

round, then weave in reverse to ladder stitch the top two rounds together (b) (Techniques, page 133).

8 Exit from the top of the herringbone tube, and pick up 2 size 11 ruby. Skipping the nearest bridge of thread between beads, stitch under the following thread, moving toward you, and pull snug. Stitch up through the second seed bead just added.

9 Pick up 1 size 11 ruby and stitch under the next thread bridge in the tube. Pull snug, and stitch up through the bead just added. Repeat to add 2 more beads.

10 Stitch down through the first bead added in step 8 and through the following 2 beads in the herringbone tube. Pass the needle between beads in the tube, and exit from the opening at the top.

11 String on 1 topaz spacer and 13 size 11 topaz seed beads. Stitch down through the first

topaz bead added and the spacer, then exit between beads in the herringbone tube. Pull snug to form a loop at the top of the beadwork.

12 Stitch down through the nearest 2 seed beads in the tube and up through the following 2, using the existing herringbone thread path. Pass the needle between beads and up through the spacer. Weave through the loop once more, and exit from the tube again. Stitch down through the nearest column of beads to exit from the lowest size 11 ruby in this section.

13 Pick up 7 size 11 ruby seed beads. Count up 4 beads in the column, then stitch down through those 4 beads to form a loop. Pull snug, then pass through the 7 beads just added again and up through the nearest ruby seed bead in the tube.

14 Following the herringbone thread path, weave across 3 columns in the tube to

exit from the lowest size 11 ruby on the opposite side. Repeat step 13 to add a second loop of 7 seed beads.

15 Weave in the remaining thread, passing through each 7-bead loop once, then through the larger bead rounds to tighten the beadwork. Secure the thread in a size 11 section and trim.

16 Using the tail thread, repeat steps 8 to 10 on the opposite end of the tube. Pick up 1 topaz spacer and 1 size 11 topaz. Pass back through the spacer and into the tube, exiting between beads. Weave through a few beads in the column and pass through the spacer again. Secure any remaining thread and trim.

17 String the amphora pendant on a 32-in. (81-cm) length of waxed cotton cord. Secure the cord ends with sliding knots, then glue and trim the tails.

7a

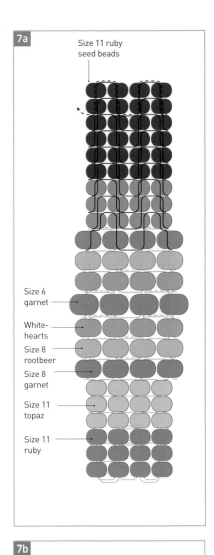

Size 11 ruby seed beads

Size 6 garnet

White-hearts

Size 8 rootbeer

Size 8 garnet

Size 11 topaz

Size 11 ruby

7b

8

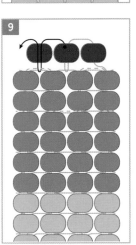

9

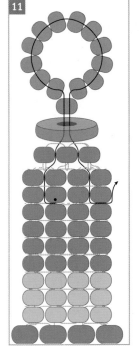

10

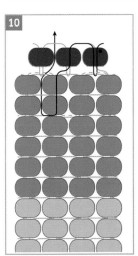

11

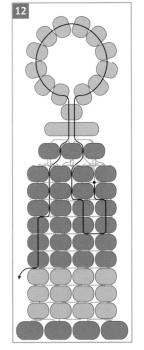

12

13

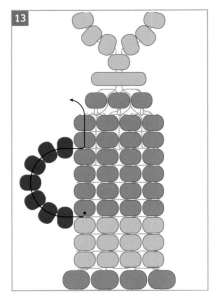

14

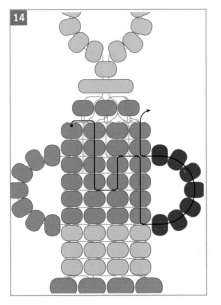

16

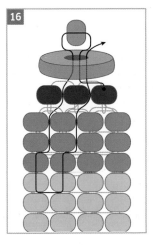

Variations: There is just enough space in the center of the tube to hide a small treasure or secret message. To make your pendant really mystical, tuck in a crystal or tiny scroll before decreasing the tube to size 11 beads again in step 7.

Core Techniques

These core techniques will help you to complete the designs in this book. Some projects will refer to these pages for essential stitches and knots. As some techniques can vary in application, even if you're already familiar with the stitch, check these pages to be sure that the approach will apply to your current project.

THREAD AND CORD BASICS

Most of the projects in this book will begin with a standard 2-yd (1.8-m) length of thread. When adding new lengths of thread to an existing project, cut a strand that is no longer than your wingspan (the length of your outstretched arms). Thread your needles from the outside end, not the end just cut from the spool.

STOP BEADS AND TAILS
At the start of some projects, and whenever you need to add new thread, you'll need to attach a stop bead (also known as a lock bead). To do this, pick up a size 11 seed bead in a color that contrasts with your project and slide it down to the end of the thread. Pass up through the bead again and gently pull tight to hold the bead in place. The remaining thread, or tail, will be worked into your project once stitching is complete—be sure to leave the correct length for each project. In most cases, a 6-in. (15-cm) tail is more than enough for a new thread.

ADDING NEW THREAD
To incorporate a new thread into your beadwork, enter a bead at least ½ in. (1 cm) back from where your previous thread was exiting (you may want to leave the working thread in place until your new thread is secured). Weave through the beadwork, following the natural path of threads already stitched until you exit from the correct bead.

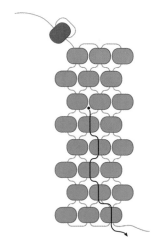

WEAVING IN THREAD
To secure your threads and strengthen your beadwork, weave all ends and tails in for a minimum of 3 in. (7.5 cm). Move along the natural thread path of the beadwork, and cross over your tails at least once before trimming. To get an even distribution, weave the ends of your working thread toward the start of the beadwork, and weave tails from new threads toward the end.

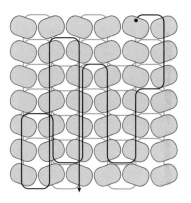

HALF-HITCH KNOTS

Most close-stitched beadwork like herringbone or peyote does not require knotting your threads when you weave them in—so long as you weave in securely. Loose stitches like netting or stringing should be knotted for extra durability. To tie off threads with a half-hitch knot, pass the needle under a thread in the beadwork, and pull most of the way to form a loop. Pass the needle through the loop, and carefully pull snug to form a knot on the base thread. Continue weaving through at least 1½ in. (4 cm) of beadwork before trimming.

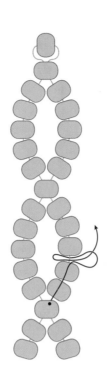

SQUARE KNOT

This essential beading knot is a lot like a shoelace knot. To tie, wrap one thread over the other once. Then bring the ends together and cross over a second time. Pull snug so that the knot tightens close to your work.

SLIDING KNOTS

This adjustable closure is always done in pairs for an easy-to-wear, clasp-free design.

1 To tie, lay the ends of your cord so that they overlap slightly.

2 Fold about 5 in. (12.5 cm) of one cord end, forming a loop with the second cord end passing underneath.

3 Hold the loop and opposite cord together with one hand, and use the other to wrap the first end around both remaining cords three times.

4 Tuck the tag end under and through the loop, passing under the base cord. Hold the tag with one hand, and use the other to steadily push the wraps toward the tag end, closing the loop and forming a tight knot.

5 Turn the cords and use the other tail end to form a second knot, just like the first. Trim the tails about ⅛ in. (3 mm) from the knots. Dab the tail ends and the base of the tails with a small amount of clear nail polish to prevent fraying.

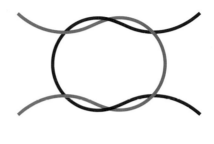

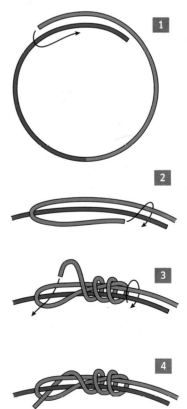

HERRINGBONE WEAVE

1 For an easy first row and a smooth edge, begin herringbone weave with a 2-bead ladder. Thread a needle on 2 yd (1.8 m) of beading line and pick up 4 size 11 seed beads. Slide them down to the end, leaving a tail of 6 in. (15 cm) or more.

2 Stitch up through the first 2 beads again, and pull snug. You should have 2 pairs of beads stacked side by side. Stitch down through the second pair of beads, and pull the thread snug.

3 Pick up 2 beads and pass down through the second stack again. Each time you add a new pair of beads, you will stitch toward your thread. Pull the thread snug, and the new beads should stack up next to the previous pair.

4 Stitch up through the 2 new beads again and pull tight. Pick up 2 beads and pass back up through the last 2 beads added and then down through the 2 new beads. Continue adding 2 beads at a time until your ladder is the desired width. You will need an even number of columns for any herringbone pattern.

5 Step up to begin the first herringbone row by stitching up through the lower bead of the previous column and then through the top bead of the last column.

6 Pick up 2 size 11 seed beads. Stitch down through the top bead of the previous column and up through the following top bead (a). Pull snug to bring the 2 new beads side by side on the 2 columns. Repeat across the edge, and step up on a diagonal as before (b).

7 Flip the beadwork to weave the next row from right to left. Repeat until you have a herringbone strip of the desired length.

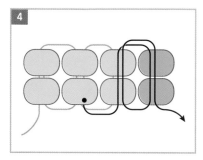

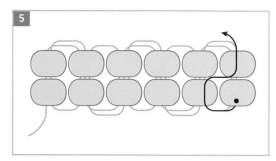

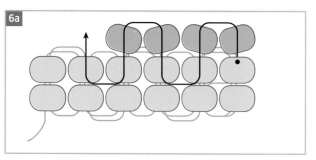

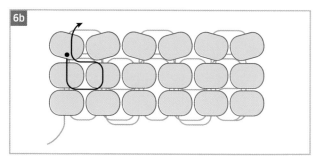

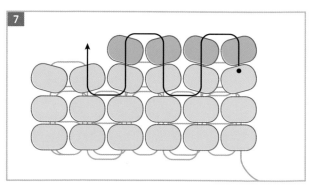

TUBULAR HERRINGBONE

To make a herringbone rope or tube, begin by lashing your base ladder into a ring.

1 Add the final column in the ladder, then stitch up through the first column and down through the one just added to join the edges.

2 Weave through the same beads once more to secure, then up through 1 more column to exit from the opposite side from your tail thread.

3 Add 2 beads at a time as usual around the edge.

4 To step up at the end of each round, pass up through the top 2 beads of the first column in the ring.

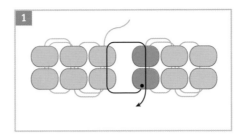

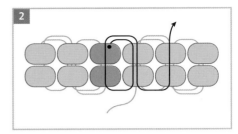

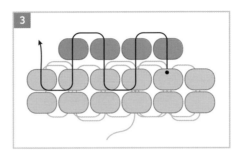

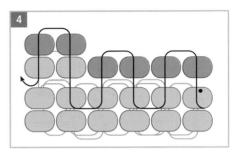

HERRINGBONE DUMMY STITCH

To close up the final rows and make a smooth edge, work 1 row of herringbone without picking up any beads.

1 Pass down through the topmost bead of the previous column and up through the top bead of the next column. Repeat across the edge.

2 Instead of a regular step up, exit the second column from the end. Stitch down through the previous column to join the beads together and mimic the previous ladder stitch start. Stitch up through the following column and repeat across the edge.

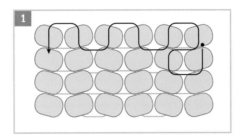

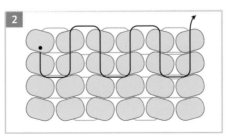

PEYOTE STITCH TOGGLE

1 Thread a needle on 1 yd (0.9 m) of beading line and attach a stop bead to the end with a 6-in. (15-cm) tail. Pick up 12 size 11 seed beads and slide them down to the stop bead.

2 Flip the strand so that the tail thread is facing away from you and gently hold the last few beads added with your other hand, with just enough space to needle through. Pick up 1 size 11 bead. Skipping the last bead in the strand, stitch through the next bead, and gently pull the thread snug.

3 Pick up 1 bead. Pass over the next bead in the strand and stitch through the following bead. Pull snug. Continue adding 1 bead at a time to every other bead in the strand, until you exit from the other side.

4 Flip the beadwork. Pick up 1 bead, and stitch up through the first raised bead—the last one added in the previous row. Pull snug. Continue adding 1 bead at a time in this manner, flipping the beadwork at the end of each row, until you have a peyote panel 4 beads wide.

5 Remove the stop bead, weave in the tail thread, and trim. Pick up the working thread again, and fold the long edges of the panel together so that the raised beads alternate evenly. Needle through the first bead in the opposite side of the tube and then across the gap into the first raised bead of the other side. Pull the thread snug to lock the beads together.

6 Needle through the second raised bead in the opposite side and the next raised bead across the gap. Pull snug. Continue zigzagging back and forth across the gap to zip up the tube.

7 Join the last 2 beads, exit from the edge, and then stitch down through the final bead in the opposite side to close the tube. Weave across the join to exit from the opposite side.

8 Pick up 3 size 11 seed beads, and stitch down through the top bead of the next row in the tube edge (a). Pull snug to form a picot. Stitch up through the top bead of the next row and repeat (b).

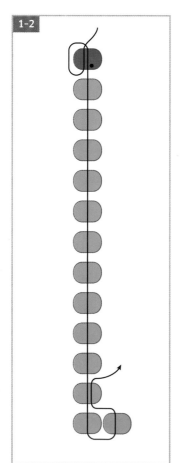

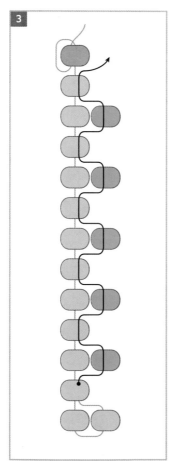

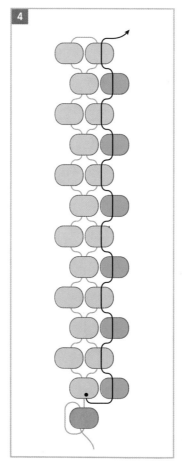

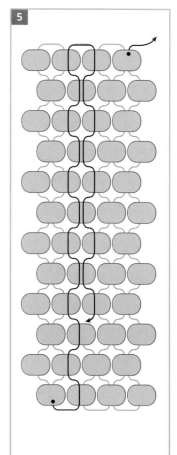

9 Exit from the first bead added in the original picot. Pick up 1 size 11 bead, and stitch down through the second bead of the opposite picot. Weave around and repeat on the other side.

10 Stitch up through the beadwork to exit from the center bead of the nearest picot. Weave around all 4 center beads twice, then weave across the tube.

11 Repeat steps 8 through 10 to finish the other edge with picots. Secure any remaining thread in the tube and trim.

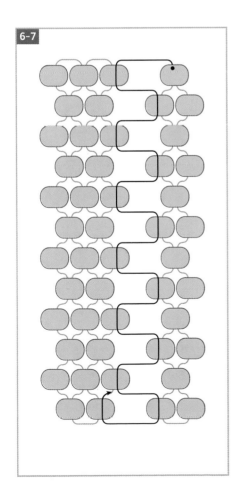

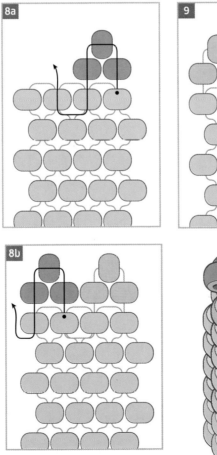

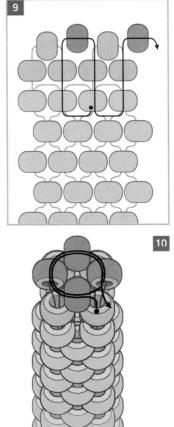

PEARL NET BEADED BEADS

1 Cut 30 in. (76 cm) of beading line and string a size 11 seed bead and a 4 mm round bead. Repeat 3 times. Slide all of the beads down to the end of the thread, leaving a 6-in. (15-cm) tail.

2 Pass through all of the beads again, and gently pull the thread tight to form a ring of 8 beads. Pass through the first 3 beads again to exit from a size 11, and pull tight.

3 Pick up 4 size 15, 1 size 11, and 4 more size 15 seed beads. Stitch through the following size 11 seed bead in the first round, and pull tight (a). Repeat 3 times so that there is a net above each round bead in the base round (b). Pass through the first 5 beads added in this round to step up.

4 Pick up a 6 mm round bead and pass through the following size 11 bead from the netting round. Pull snug and hold the beadwork steady to keep the tension even. Repeat 3 times.

5 Pass through the first 6 mm bead added in step 4 and the following size 11 seed bead to step up. Pick up 4 size 15, 1 size 11, and 4 size 15 seed beads. Stitch through the following size 11 seed bead between the 6 mm beads, and pull snug. Repeat 3 times.

6 Pass through the first 5 beads added in this round to step up. Pick up a 4 mm round bead and stitch through the next size 11 bead. Repeat 3 times.

7 Weave through all of the 4 mm beads and size 11 seed beads in the top round to secure them, then stitch down through 4 size 15 seed beads and into the 6-mm round bead. Weave around the beadwork at least once through all of the pearls and then through the top round of netting. Exit from between 2 size 15 seed beads, and trim the thread.

8 Thread a needle on the tail and reinforce the first row of 4 mm beads and the first row of netting. Trim the thread.

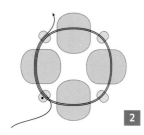

2

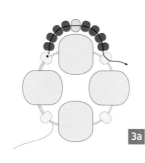

3a

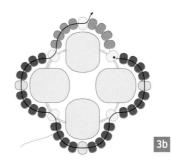

3b

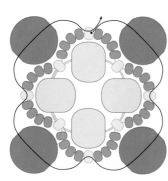

4

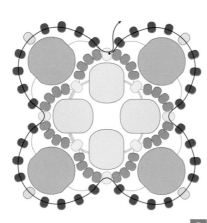

5

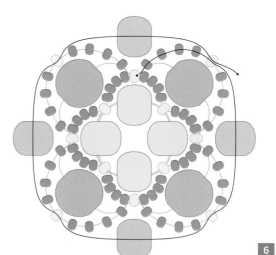

6

CIRCULAR BRICK STITCH

1 Thread a needle on 1 yd (0.9 m) of beading line, and slide a 6 mm round bead to the end, leaving a 6-in. (15-cm) tail. Stitch up through the bead 4 times, forming a double loop of thread all the way around the bead.

2 Pick up 2 size 11 seed beads. Bring the needle under the 2 bridge threads, moving toward you. Pull snug so that the beads rest side by side and stitch up through the second bead added, being careful not to snag or cross the threads. The beads should now be locked in place.

3 Pick up 1 size 11 seed bead. Bring the needle under the bridge thread, toward you, and pull snug to position the new bead next to the first 2 beads. Stitch up through the bead just added.

4 Continue adding 1 seed bead at a time all the way around the 6 mm bead. When you have added the last bead, close the gap between the first and last seed beads by stitching down through the first bead added in the round and up through the bead just added. Stitch down through the first bead again and up through the second bead added this round.

5 Pick up 2 seed beads to begin the next round. Bring the needle under the nearest bridge thread between 2 beads and pull snug to position the 2 new beads. Stitch up through the second bead just added.

6 Continue the round with 1 bead per stitch, using the threads connecting the beads in the first round as your bridge. Close the round in the same way as the first, and step up to begin a new round. To prevent the beadwork from curving into a concave shape, always use the nearest available bridge, even if it has a bead stitched on already.

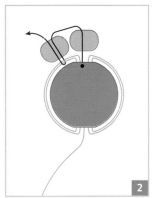

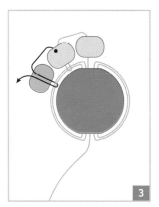

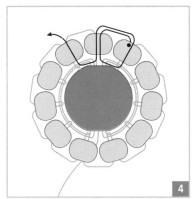

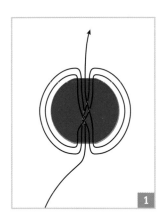

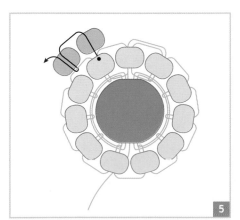

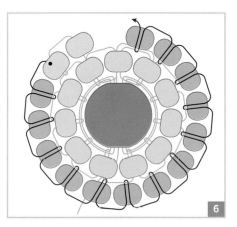

BRICK STITCH BUTTON TRIM

To make a brick stitch button, work a minimum of 3 rounds with size 11 seed beads.

PICOT TRIM

Close the last round of circular brick stitch (page 137) and pick up 3 size 11 seed beads. Pass under the nearest bridge and stitch up through the last bead just added. Add 2 beads per stitch for the rest of the round, stitching up through the second bead. To close the round, pick up 1 bead and stitch down through the first bead added in the round, and up through the second bead added in the previous stitch. Secure any remaining thread in the beadwork and trim.

SQUARE STITCH TRIM

Close the last round of brick stitch (page 137), and hold the beadwork on its side, with the tail facing away from you. Pick up 1 size 8 bead, stitch under the nearest bridge thread, and pull snug so that the new bead rests perpendicular to the beadwork. Stitch up through the bead just added, and pull snug. Repeat all the way around the edge, then weave through all of the size 8 beads twice and secure any remaining thread in the brick stitch.

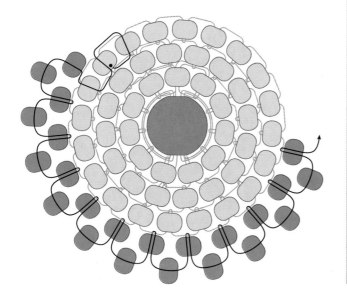
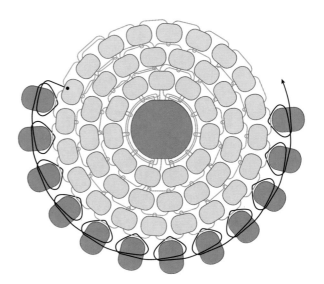

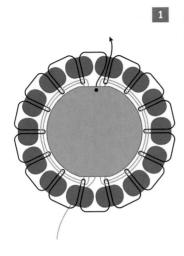 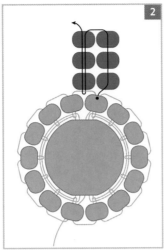 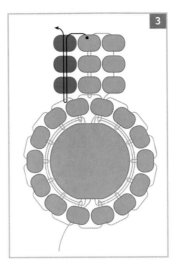 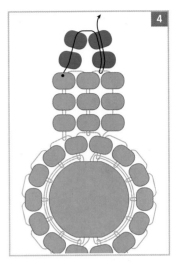

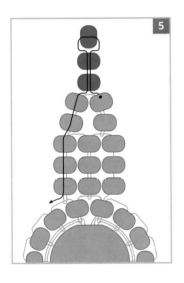 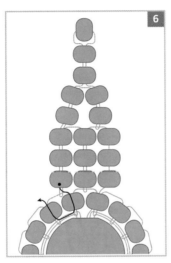 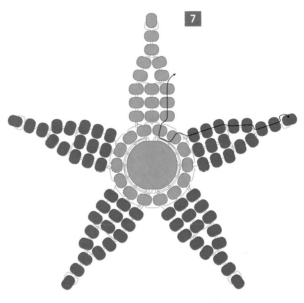

STARFISH BEADED BEADS

1 Thread a 6-mm druk bead on 30 in. (76 cm) of braided beading line, leaving a 6-in. (15-cm) tail. Stitch up through the druk 4 times to create a double bridge of thread around the bead. Add a single round of circular brick stitch with size 15 seed beads (page 137), and step up. Your base round will need at least 14 beads, so take care to stitch with even tension and spacing.

2 Pick up 6 size 15 seed beads. Moving right to left, bring the needle under the nearest bridge of thread between 2 beads in the base row and pull snug. The new beads should form 2 stacks of 3, side by side. Stitch up through the last 3 beads added.

3 Pick up 3 size 15 seed beads, and pass under the nearest thread bridge. Pull snug, and stitch up through all of the beads just added.

4 Pick up 4 seed beads. Moving from left to right, bring the needle under the farthest bridge thread at the top of the three bead stacks. Pull snug and stitch up through the last 2 beads just added.

5 Pick up 3 beads. Skipping the third bead added, stitch down through the first 2 beads and the following 2 beads on the left of the previous row. Stitch down through the following 3 beads on the left side of the first row added.

6 Stich down through the nearest bead in the base row, to the left of the row your thread is exiting. Stitch up through the next bead in the base to step up.

7 Repeat steps 2 through 6 to add 4 more starfish arms. The final arm will be very snug to the first one added and will share beads in the base row. Weave in any remaining thread and the tail, and trim.

Ring Size Guide

A ring-sizing mandrel is an excellent tool to have in your workspace—the tapered shape is ideal for safely stretching your finished pieces, and the ruled side provides perfect sizing results every time. If you're not ready to invest in a mandrel just yet, the following charts can help you to measure your beadwork to get the ring size that you need.

To measure your beadwork, simply place it over the appropriate diagram to gauge its size, and adjust as needed. Start your measurements early, so you can work up to the size you want, rather than removing stitches to downsize.

   You can also measure an existing ring on the circular table below to determine its size, then make your beadwork project to match.

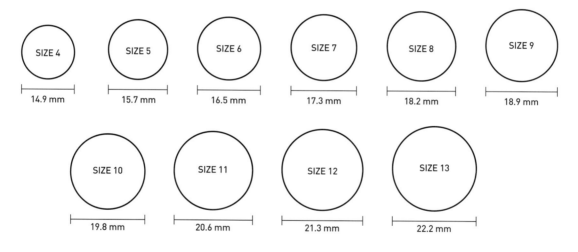

SIZE 4	SIZE 5	SIZE 6	SIZE 7	SIZE 8	SIZE 9
14.9 mm	15.7 mm	16.5 mm	17.3 mm	18.2 mm	18.9 mm

SIZE 10	SIZE 11	SIZE 12	SIZE 13
19.8 mm	20.6 mm	21.3 mm	22.2 mm

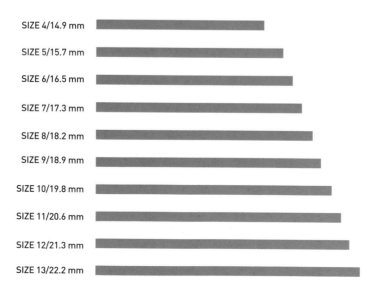

SIZE 4/14.9 mm
SIZE 5/15.7 mm
SIZE 6/16.5 mm
SIZE 7/17.3 mm
SIZE 8/18.2 mm
SIZE 9/18.9 mm
SIZE 10/19.8 mm
SIZE 11/20.6 mm
SIZE 12/21.3 mm
SIZE 13/22.2 mm

Remember that your beadwork can stretch a little or a lot, depending on the techniques you've used to make the band. By making your ring smaller than desired, then stretching it on a dowel or mandrel, you can prevent your finished rings from changing size over time. Follow the instructions given in each project to achieve the correct size after stretching.

Resources

BEADS AND MATERIALS

Some bead shops and craft supply stores will carry most or all of the materials you'll need to complete the projects in this book. If your local bead shop doesn't carry a product you need, they may be able to order it for you. Online shops also offer a convenient way to browse for absolutely anything you require to make a project fabulous. Here are a few of my favorite places for stocking up that offer worldwide shipping.

HappyMangoBeads.com
This store specializes in unique imported beads. If you want something handmade, rustic, organic, or unusual, Happy Mango is likely to have it. Stock can vary, but you're sure to find a great selection of Java glass, wood, pearls, and even Ancient Roman glass.

Artbeads.com
If you're just getting your bead stash started, Artbeads is a great place to stock up on the basics.

There is an easy-to-browse catalog of Japanese seed beads, glass and crystal, threads, tools, and more. The selection is excellent without being overwhelming.

ArtFire.com and Etsy.com
Independent bead sellers who list on these crafty sites often have beads that you can't find anywhere else. If you're looking for a rare Czech glass shape or just the right strand of freshwater pearls, you can probably find it on Etsy or ArtFire. You can also browse for bead sellers in your area and shop local.

FireMountainGems.com
This website has a vast selection of beads, threads, findings, tools, and other jewelry-making materials. Pricing is set by tiered volume discounts, making Fire Mountain Gems a great stop when you're ready to fully stock your bead stash.

When shopping for seed beads, glass, and crystal be sure to check the labels for a country of origin or brand. If it isn't listed, there's a good chance that the contents are of generic quality.

Seed beads are made in batches, and colors can sometimes vary from batch to batch. If you're buying seed beads for a specific project, it's a good idea to get extra, just in case. You never know if you'll be able to get that exact color or finish again.

INSPIRATION

Many of the designs featured in this book are inspired by real artifacts from the classical world. If you're looking for your own unique inspirations from the past but can't visit an exhibit up close, check out the online collections of these famous museums.

www.Metmuseum.org
The Metropolitan Museum of Art in New York City first opened its doors in 1870. It holds one of the most prestigious collections of classical artifacts, including over 26,000 Egyptian antiquities, and 17,000 Greek and Roman artworks. Visit the Collection tab on the home page to see highlights, or search by keyword.

www.Britishmuseum.org
The British Museum was the world's first national public museum, and has been offering free admission to visitors since 1753. It is home to many important classical pieces such as the Rosetta Stone from Egypt, and the Parthenon Sculptures from Athens. Visit the Explore page to browse collections or search for artifacts by category.

www.SMB.Museum
The Berlin State Museums is a group of several museums, libraries, and institutes—including the Neues Museum, the current home of the bust of Nefertiti. Check out the Research tab on the home page to access the online catalog and database of items in the group's collections.

For help with basic beading techniques or questions about the designs in this book, please visit my blog Inspirational Beading. You'll find tutorials for core techniques, color tips, beading ideas, and more at InspirationalBeading. blogspot.com

Index

Credits

Many thanks go to Cyrus and Shane, my wonderful family, for supporting me in so many ways during the completion of this book. Thanks also to my fantastic blog readers for all of their patience throughout this journey, and to the talented teams at Quarto for their ideas and hard work. I couldn't have done it without any of you.

Special thanks to Elaine Partington, who provided the fabric backgrounds on pages 54, 72, 94, and 98; and to Matthew Durran, who handmade the glass backgrounds on pages 2, 4, 6, 16, 21, 38, 48, 86, 118, and 122.

Quarto would like to thank the following for providing images for inclusion in this book:
(t = top)

© Aerelon, istockphoto.com, p.43t
© INTERFOTO/Alamy, p.98t
© PRISMA ARCHIVO/Alamy, p.69
© The Metropolitan Museum of Art/Art Resource/Scala, Florence, pp.19t, 107t
© World History Archive/Alamy, pp.3, 64t
© www.BibleLandPictures.com/Alamy, p.95
Abxyz, Shutterstock.com, p.54t
BasPhoto, Shutterstock.com, p.28t
Christian Musat, Shutterstock.com, p.82
Getty Images, pp.16t, 61t, 87t, 123t
Gts, Shutterstock.com, p107t
Inacio Pires, Shutterstock.com, p.119t
Kamira, Shutterstock.com, p.103t
Leoks, Shutterstock.com, pp.31t, 39t
Mauro Rodrigues, Shutterstock.com, p.73t
MIGUEL GARCIA SAAVEDRA, Shutterstock.com, p.57t
Mountainpix, Shutterstock.com, p.49t
Myroslava, Shutterstock.com, p.78t
Netfalls, Remy Musser, Shutterstock.com, p.25t
Oleg Senkov, Shutterstock.com, p.100t
Only Fabrizio, Shutterstock.com, p.127t
Philip Pilosian, Shutterstock.com, p.115t
Sergieiev, Shutterstock.com, p.34t
Tkachuk, Shutterstock.com, p.21t